ENGLISH ✛ HERIT

Book of
Channel Defences

ENGLISH ☐ HERITAGE

Book of
Channel
Defences

Andrew Saunders

B. T. Batsford / English Heritage
London

© Andrew Saunders 1997

First published 1997

Typeset by Bernard Cavender Design & Greewood Graphics Publishing
Printed and bound in Great Britain by
The Bath Press, Bath

Published by B.T. Batsford Ltd
583 Fulham Road, London SW6 5BY

A CIP catalogue record for this book is
available from the British Library

ISBN 0 7134 7594 3 (cased)
0 7134 7595 1 (limp)

(Front cover) The battlements of fifteenth-century
Dartmouth Castle, one of the earliest of English coastal
defences designed for artillery (© *English Heritage*).

(Back cover) A 38-ton rifled muzzle-loading gun in one of
the nineteenth-century casemates at Hurst Castle
(© *English Heritage*).

Contents

Illustrations

Colour plates

Acknowledgements

I should like to thank a number of institutions who have supplied illustrations and who have given permission for their reproduction: The British Library (**4, 50, 51, 55**); Public Record Office (**39, 53**); National Maritime Museum (**5, 8, 25, colour plates 3, 4, 5, 10**); Imperial War Museum (**38, 76, 82, 84, 85**); Royal Engineers Library, Chatham (**30, 44, 65, 66**); Hatfield House (**26, 33**); Society of Antiquaries of London (**3, 24**); Royal Commission on the Historical Monuments of England (**34, 43**); Tate Gallery (**colour plate 2**); Hulton/Deutsch (**7**); Aerofilms (**40**); Eastbourne Museum (**58**); Frances Griffith, Devon County Council (**48**); and the Cornwall Archaeological Unit (**49, 83**). I am especially grateful to fellow members of the Fortress Study Group: Victor T.C. Smith (**11, 17, 28**), John Goodwin (**12**) and the late Peter Sprack (**42**) for photographs and drawings; Philip A. Magrath (**35**) and especially to Chris Evans for his maps and reconstructions (**1, 2, 9, 10, 21, 29, 32, 41, 47, 57, 59, 60**). The English Heritage photographic library was particularly helpful (**19, 20, 22, 23, 61, 62, 67, 68, colour plates 1, 6, 7, 8, 9, 11, 12**). My general editor, Stephen Johnson, gave much good advice and corrected errors; he, Peter Kemmis Betty and Charlotte Vickerstaff of Batsford offered encouragement throughout.

Preface

During the past five hundred years many defensive measures have been taken to protect the coasts of England from invasion and disruptive raids. These measures have left much in the way of physical remains: some on a large scale, others more ephemeral. This book is an attempt to identify the range of what survives along the south and south-east coasts, to put it into its broad historical and topographical context, and to describe some of its more significant components.

This cannot be a general history of the defence of Britain against invasion, nor is it a history of fortification as such and the effect that changing weapon technologies have had on its development, though these will become apparent. It is rather a review of the impact that fortification has had on the historical landscape and shoreline of the Channel coasts since the reign of Henry VIII and a description of many of those sites which can be visited today. It is concerned with the questions of why forts and batteries are where they are, how they functioned and how they have changed to meet new forms of attack. In some respects these 'modern' fortifications are part of a progression from the prehistoric coastal promontory forts, the Roman forts of the 'Saxon Shore' and medieval castles. Sometimes there is continuity in the defensive use of a particular topographical feature (**colour plate 1**).

Gunpowder artillery fortification and its derivatives can occasionally still have the visual and architectural impact of the castle. Elsewhere it may have a more elusive quality, especially in the precautions taken against German invasion in 1940. Generally, it must be said, that as structures with distinct functions, their aesthetic qualities are usually limited. Coastal defences are here seen primarily in terms of their surviving structures, technical developments and changing functions set against the intermittent threat of external enemies.

The Channel was often described as England's moat – natural defensive barrier – but, paradoxically, the sea is also a highway giving an enemy the freedom and mobility to raid the coasts at will, even if he stopped short of full-scale invasion and military conquest. A navy was essential to meet the threat head-on and to patrol the seaways. Measures to guard against landward attack were necessary both at local level and within an evolving defence strategy, requiring both military and naval forces which could only be the responsibility of central government. Henry VIII was the first monarch to consider coastal fortifications on a national scale in the face of the danger of invasion. He was not the last. While there was always an underlying feeling of insecurity among coastal communities, there were times when more serious invasion threats, real and sometimes imagined, were perceived by the country as a whole. That danger was most conspicuous in the summer of 1940.

It is by no means fanciful to regard coastal defences in archaeological terms. The structures themselves often show continuity of purpose as well as change and modification over time. The historic landscape in which they were set changed too. The Kent and Sussex coasts have become blurred over centuries. The shifting sands and silting rivers have altered the topography so much that the old harbours of the Cinque Ports either no longer exist or have ceased to have any maritime significance. Camber Castle stands in a sea of shingle; the harbour it once protected disappeared in the seventeenth century. Elsewhere, such as in Pevensey Bay, the development of yacht marinas and associated housing, caravan sites as well as expanding suburbs, have made a nonsense of this part of the Napoleonic invasion coast. Martello towers may now be seen as traffic islands amid housing estates. The anti-tank obstacles and pillboxes of 1940 have nearly all been bulldozed away. Emergency batteries have become replaced by the sea walls of a coast defence against natural forces. To discover former fortification in many parts of the Channel coast and its hinterland requires acute observation and fieldwork; some of the most recent can only be traced through the process of aerial photography. While the patterns of coastal defence have often to be sought out, even the early twentieth-century airfields of 'The Battle of Britain' are becoming a transient feature. The surviving remains therefore become more and more important to the understanding of an outstanding event in the history of Britain.

It must be accepted that Britain's defences against foreign aggression have, until the Second World War, rested primarily on the Royal Navy. During much of the twentieth century the Royal Air Force occupied the front line; though in more recent years the key role seems to have returned to the navy with its sea-to-air missiles operated by Polaris and Trident submarines. With the development of aircraft in the twentieth century, a new dimension was added to warfare. This new dimension, too, has had its effect upon the development of the historic landscape and has made its own archaeological impact.

Traditionally, the standing army has been small in number and a professional body. Its role was for long directed towards operations beyond the British Isles, whether in continental campaigns or establishing empire, leaving much of home defence to the militia and local volunteer forces. The fixed fortifications, which were manned by the regular army or by volunteers, were essentially the second line of national defence – whether they were for the protection of the dockyards and shore establishments of the navy or for resisting enemy landings on the beaches and attacks on coastal towns and ports.

There have been those navalists, particularly during the nineteenth century, the so-called 'Blue Water School', who have claimed that the navy was the only real defence against invasion and all expenditure on permanent fortification was superfluous and wasteful. Others, while acknowledging that the primary defence of the Channel coasts must lie with the navy, have feared that from time to time the navy could temporarily lose control of the Narrow Seas or be lured away by enemy manoeuvre, thereby providing an opportunity for an invading force to make a landing. Therefore it was prudent to have that second line of permanent defence on the coast. This was the 'Bolt from the Blue School'. In any case, the navy's bases and dockyards themselves needed protection whether from seaward attack or from a landing-party aiming for a destructive raid on the ships at their moorings or upon the dockyard installations.

Although the book relates to the Channel coast, which is defined for this purpose as extending from the Isles of Scilly in the west to the approaches to the Thames and Medway rivers in the south-east and sometimes as far as Harwich, it is inevitable that it has to be put into the wider setting of British defensive preparations over the centuries (**1**). There is therefore a chapter identifying the particular occasions when danger of invasion threatened and the direction from which it came. In the first half of the sixteenth century the threat was focused principally on the south-east corner of England; by the end of the century it passed to the south-west. It shifted briefly to the east coasts during the seventeenth-century wars with the Dutch before returning to the south-east in the face of the traditional hostility

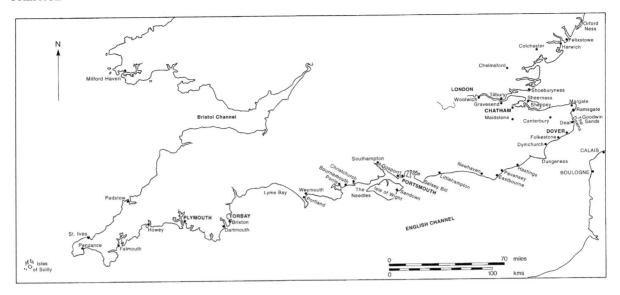

1 *Map of the English Channel from the Isles of Scilly to Harwich indicating the main ports and anchorages.*

with France. During the First World War the menaced coasts were on the eastern side of England and Scotland because the source of the threat had shifted to Germany, but in the Second World War the hostile occupation of the whole of the European seaboard from the Pyrenees to the North Cape magnified the threat as never before.

Another chapter discusses how the Royal Navy organized its primary responsibilities in home waters over the years and how it lived up to its role. The chapters on the coast defences themselves are divided between those fixed fortifications protecting the naval dockyards and the main anchorages from those, often temporary works, erected in the urgency and alarm of an actual invasion threat. The complexities of warfare through two world wars as they affected coastal and air defence in the twentieth century have required a chapter of their own.

Coastal defence was officially abolished in 1956. This book is an overview of 500 years in the fortification of the Channel coast against invasion. While parallels may be drawn from other parts of the country, the examples which are here described in some detail are those fortifications associated with the south and south-east coasts and which are now the most accessible and visually rewarding.

1
Times of danger

The times when Britain was in danger of invasion over the last five centuries are surprisingly numerous. One was successful in 1688 when William of Orange showed what was possible with a small force if the Royal Navy could be evaded. Otherwise there were eleven actual attempts and at least nine occasions when preparations were begun but came to nothing. In addition, there were many invasion scares real or imaginary which seized the popular imagination, especially in the nineteenth century, ironically during the height of Britain's imperial power. Invasion and occupation of the British Isles was the theme of a number of novels of which Erskine Childers' *The Riddle of the Sands* (1903) is the best known. There is still an invasion literature to the present day.

Cross-Channel raiding was frequent during the Middle Ages and especially during the Hundred Years War. The Sussex town of Rye was sacked and burnt in 1339, 1377, 1385 and 1448; Hastings in 1339 and 1377; Winchelsea in 1360 and 1380. There were similar destructive raids elsewhere along the south coast. Defensive measures were put in place usually after the damage had been done. Thus the decision to complete the circuit of Southampton's walls along the waterside was only taken after the disastrous French raid in 1338. The new defences were constructed and improved fitfully during the second half of the fourteenth century, becoming gradually adapted for the use of gunpowder artillery. Even in *c.* 1365 the abbey of Quarr on the Isle of Wight had a stone precinct wall equipped with gunports, the earliest known in England.

Raids, which were destructive but not intended to be long-term seizure of territory, continued into later centuries. The French attempt on Henry VIII's naval base of Portsmouth in 1545 led to a two-day occupation of the Isle of Wight. The Spaniards caused havoc with their landings in west Cornwall in 1595. The most damaging of all, materially and politically, was the Dutch raid on the Thames Estuary and the Medway in 1667. The French attacked Jersey in 1779 and 1781 (**colour plate 2**) and there were slightly earlier descents upon Ireland and Pembrokeshire. In more recent times the shelling of Hartlepool, Whitby and Scarborough in 1914 was more an act of terrorism than an attack on a naval or military target, while indiscriminate aerial bombardment of civilian populations, which began during the First World War, was converted into a deliberate and widespread strategic objective during the Second World War by both sides.

A more subtle form of attack was blockade and the disturbance of seaborne trade. This was elaborated into a major element of British naval policy during the Napoleonic wars with France. With the arrival of the submarine, the inshore mine and the fast surface raider, Britain herself was especially vulnerable. In both world wars these forms of attack on merchant shipping were equivalent to a siege of a castle with starvation and economic ruin as the objective.

Henry VIII

It has been said that 'the only successful invasion of England in Tudor times was the one that established the Tudors themselves as a dynasty'. Henry Tudor's challenge to the Yorkist dynasty began with a landing in Pembrokeshire and was resolved at Bosworth Field in 1485. Other landings by Henry VII's rivals came to nothing.

Actual invasion threatened in 1538–9, sparked by Henry VIII's divorce of Catherine of Aragon and Henry's assumption of the title of Head of the Church in England. A peace treaty was drawn up between England's traditional enemy, France, and the Holy Roman Emperor Charles V of Spain, Catherine's nephew. The pope hoped for a crusading army to cross the Channel. Henry's ambassador in the Netherlands advised the king to guard against attack, and a spy reported on French preparations urging that 'you must fortify your places and harbours'.

However, Charles V's enthusiasm for an invasion of England was overtaken by other problems within his empire caused by Turkish pressure on its borders and the spread of Protestantism within. The troops and ships which had been said to be massing in the Channel ports of France and the Netherlands faded away but the scare had its effect. The English agent in Venice impressed on the government that it should 'make strong and perpetual provison for the safety of the realm'. This indeed Henry did and the chronicler Edward Hall recorded that the king reviewed the preparedness of the navy and ordered musters of men fit to serve in the army to be held throughout the country and 'he sent dyvers of his nobles and counsaylours to view and search all the Portes and daungiers on the coastes where any meete or convenient landing place might be supposed... And in all suche doubtfull places his hyhnes caused dyvers & many Bulwarks & fortificacions to be made.'

The immediate threat of invasion quickly evaporated but the fortification programme continued for the remainder of Henry's reign. It was to be the largest scheme of coastal defence which had been achieved since Roman times (**2**). This

2 *(i) Locations of Henry VIII's defence works and those carried out under Edward VI. These are mostly related to anchorages and estuaries.*
(ii) Coastal-defence construction under Elizabeth. Apart from Upnor Castle and renewed fortification of Portsmouth and the Isle of Wight, emphasis moved to the south-west after 1588.
(iii) New fortifications during the Anglo-Dutch wars. Besides Plymouth, Portsmouth and Harwich, defences were concentrated on the Thames and Medway estuaries.

was a permanent measure and no temporary response to an immediate emergency. It was necessary since Henry continued his military adventures in northern France, capturing Boulogne and strengthening the English hold on Calais. The new bulwarks and blockhouses at Portsmouth and Southsea were graphically depicted in the scene of the engagement in 1545 between the French and English fleets in the Solent during which Henry's great ship, *Mary Rose*, was lost (**3**). The subsequent French landing on the Isle of Wight pointed to the vulnerability of Portsmouth as a naval base should the Isle of Wight fall into hostile hands.

During the minority of Henry's son, Edward VI, the policy of maintaining and adding to the coastal defences continued. Danger now threatened on two fronts with the French alliance with Scotland putting pressure on England's northern frontier. The loss of Calais in 1558 meant that the English crown could no more maintain its long-standing toe-hold on the continent of Europe.

The Spanish Armada

During the early years of Elizabeth's reign (1558–1603) the main threat to England's territorial security came from the north through Scotland and was countered by the new fortifications to the garrison town of Berwick-upon-Tweed. To the south, emphasis was given to the safety and efficiency of the navy whose main base was now the River Medway. The moorings in Chatham Reach, under the guns of the newly built Upnor Castle, were less vulnerable to attack and the queen's fleet was better placed for the potential

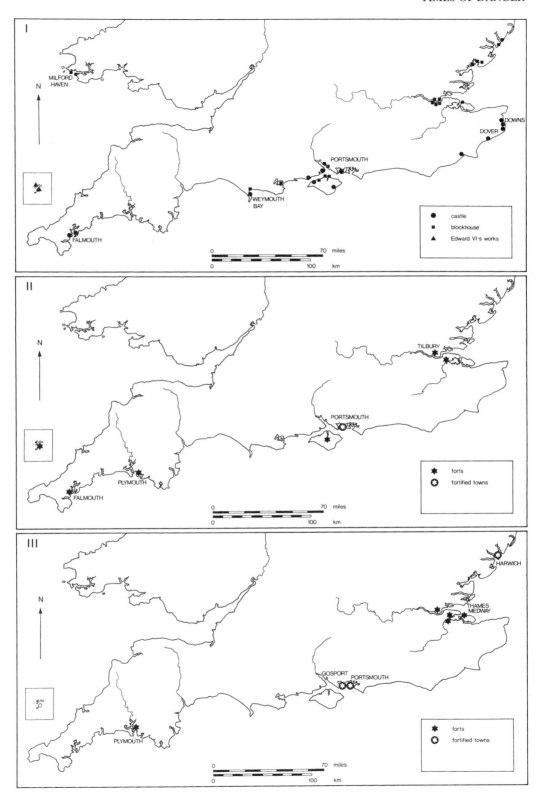

I

N

- castle
- blockhouse
- Edward VI's works

MILFORD HAVEN

DOWNS
DOVER

PORTSMOUTH

WEYMOUTH BAY

FALMOUTH

0   70 miles
0   100 km

II

N

TILBURY

PORTSMOUTH

PLYMOUTH

FALMOUTH

- forts
- fortified towns

0   70 miles
0   100 km

III

N

HARWICH

THAMES MEDWAY

GOSPORT PORTSMOUTH

PLYMOUTH

- forts
- fortified towns

0   70 miles
0   100 km

15

3 *Portsmouth: the French attack of 19 July 1545, showing the defences; including Southsea Castle, the town and Portsmouth Point as well as the loss of the* Mary Rose *in the Solent.*

threat from the Spanish Netherlands (the part of the Low Countries which is largely Belgium today) (**4** and see **5**).

Conflict with Spain became a distinct possibility after 1583. Elizabeth gave modest military support to the Dutch against the Spanish forces in the Netherlands. At the same time, English privateering in the Atlantic and Pacific endangered Spain's economic dependence on the treasure fleets. In anticipation of the Spanish reaction, attention was given to updating her father's fortifications enclosing Portsmouth.

By 1586, Philip II of Spain was determined that England should be crushed. Two proposals were put to him. His general in the Netherlands, Parma, offered to attempt an invasion using the army already there, embarking the troops in small craft. Philip's admiral, Santa Cruz, was confident that a great Spanish fleet could push its way past the English navy in the Channel to land

an army in the West Country. Because of the cost of raising 60,000 soldiers and 30,000 seamen a compromise was chosen. The main invasion force of 30,000 would be found in the Netherlands, whose crossing would be protected by the great ships of the Spanish armada, bringing with them a reinforcement of 20,000 troops from Spain. How the two forces could be brought together was not sufficiently thought through and the existence of hostile Dutch coastal craft (flyboats) meant that Parma's troop barges were at risk.

The two prongs of the impending attack were appreciated by the English government. The English fleet was divided between the western approaches of the Channel and the anchorage of the Downs. The bulk of its field army was encamped at West Tilbury close to the lowest Thames river-crossing at Gravesend so that it could oppose a landing either on the East Anglian coast or in Kent. In fact the inherent difficulties

4 *Upnor Castle in 1698 – plan and elevation following conversion into a powder magazine after the Dutch raid on the Medway.*

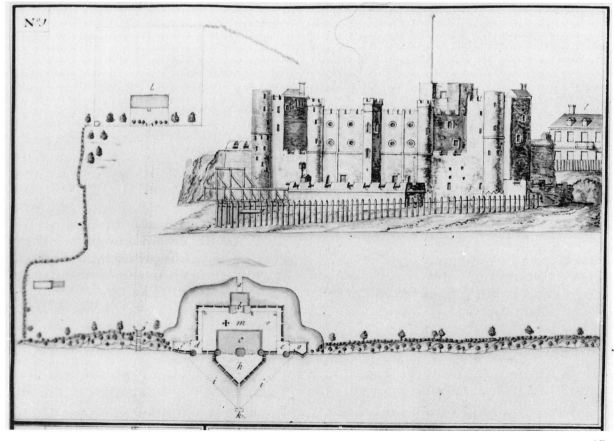

for the Spaniards in effecting a combined operation, particularly without command of the Narrow Seas, meant that the 'Enterprise of England' was doomed to failure. The deep-draughted galleons could not come close to Dunkirk because of the sandbanks, the barges could not emerge because the Dutch ships controlled the shallows and the Armada was exposed to English fireships. The long-range engagement through the Channel came to its climax with the Armada cutting its cables and scattering into the North Sea (**colour plate 3**). It was not a clear-cut English victory, even if it is agreed to be one of the decisive naval battles in world history because it helped to ensure the survival of Protestantism in Europe. In contrast, it has been described by Professor Parker as a psychological victory for Spain, for thereafter Englishmen had to regard their country as 'the beleaguered Isle'.

The defeat of the 1588 Armada in fact inaugurated a more extensive defence programme since it was justifiably believed that a new armada would soon be dispatched (see **2**). New fortifications involved the Isle of Wight, Plymouth and the Isles of Scilly. A second armada was launched in 1597 with designs on Pendennis Castle and the developing harbour of Falmouth as a western base for an invasion of England. The English fleet was this time dispersed and unable to act comprehensively, but a storm scattered the Spanish fleet when within sight of the Lizard.

Another Spanish invasion was planned in 1599 to sail from La Coruña and its orders were only countermanded because of a Dutch attack on the Canary Islands. England was now seen to be vulnerable to continental enemies. The Spanish landing in Ireland and defence of Kinsale in 1601, as part of their exploitation of an Irish rebellion against the English occupation, was confirmation of this fear.

Dutch in the Medway

James I, on his accession in 1603, set about to end the long war with Spain. Fears of invasion were now less pressing but neglect of the navy meant that the southern coasts were prey to privateers,

principally from Dunkirk, and to attacks from the North African Barbary corsairs. Little effective action was taken. In 1625, however, a dispute with Spain produced reports of great activity at Dunkirk which suggested invasion preparations were in progress. Although a false alarm, this did lead to a proposed reorganization of coastal defences in case the enemy should make an invasion attempt while the navy was engaged elsewhere.

After the Civil War in England had ended, maritime disputes developed with the Dutch over aggressive trading activities. The Parliamentary navy had grown into a coherent force and was to be an important element in the foreign policy of the Protectorate. The first Anglo-Dutch War of 1652–4, like those which continued for the next twenty years, was a naval and mercantilist conflict. These were not wars which threatened an invasion of Britain but they did strongly influence the pattern and intensity of coastal fortification (see **2**). This was concentrated on the naval dockyards and bases during the reign of Charles II (1660–85) but had earlier included the protection of anchorages in the south-west by means of gun towers at Tresco, Isles of Scilly, andthe Cattewater anchorage at Plymouth. Under Charles II the fortress construction of the 1660s and 1670s seems to have had mixed motives. There was a clear defensive objective in strengthening Portsmouth and the approaches to the Thames and Medway with forts at Tilbury and Sheerness; a retributive element in building citadels in the former Parliamentary strongholds of Plymouth and Hull; and what perhaps might be seen as an expression of another form of royal virility with the construction of expensive bastioned fortifications which aped the massive frontier defences designed by Vauban for Louis XIV.

The chief event by which the Anglo-Dutch wars are remembered is the Dutch raid on the Medway in 1667, which saw the capture or destruction of a sizeable proportion of the Royal Navy while at anchor and out of commission off Chatham (**5** and see **colour plate 5**). The new fort being built at Sheerness was burnt. There was also an attack on Landguard Fort near Harwich as well as activity in the Thames Estuary. This temporary loss of control of the Narrow Seas enabled the Dutch to continue to harry the English coasts. The effects of the Medway raid induced a loss of morale and political outrage dramatically described by Samuel Pepys.

Fear of the ambitions of Louis XIV altered the political climate, and the accession of Catholic James II pointed to an alliance with fellow Dutch Protestants. The 'Glorious Revolution' of 1688 brought William of Orange and his Stuart wife, Mary, to the throne in place of the ousted James. William's landing in Torbay showed what could be done and finished quickly by an invading army as small as 15,000 if the Royal Navy was unable to take action due to adverse weather conditions. The arrival of William of Orange was the prelude to a century of almost continuous hostility with France.

War with France 1689–1815

The intermittent warfare throughout the eighteenth century and beyond between Britain and France has been described as a 'Second Hundred Years War'. It included a succession of French invasion plans of varying complexity, some of which nearly materialized, especially in the years 1692, 1759, 1779, 1796 and 1803–5.

The French landed an army unopposed in Ireland in 1689 in support of the Stuart cause. This cause was shattered the next year at the battle of the Boyne, but an attempt was made by the large French fleet under Tourville to destroy the naval power of the English and Dutch allies. The French had initial success with the defeat off Beachy Head of the Anglo-Dutch fleet under Admiral Torrington. This traumatic result brought panic and visions of invasion. In 1692 Louis XIV indeed decided on an all-out invasion of England. The basic strategy was to land a force in Torbay before the English and Dutch ships had made their customary rendezvous. Twenty-four thousand troops were assembled in the Cotentin peninsula and transports were accumulated. Along the English south coasts defences were strengthened, the militia was raised, regular troops were encamped between

Portsmouth and Petersfield and country people were instructed to drive all cattle 15 miles inland at the point where the French fleet was sighted. With great urgency the English and Dutch fleets were united and as a result the invasion plans were aborted. Acting to orders, Tourville's much smaller fleet nevertheless attacked, anticipating pro-Jacobite desertions among the English contingent. The subsequent decisive English victory at Barfleur-La Hogue significantly ended serious danger for a further thirty years.

This is not to say that no other invasion schemes were put forward. In 1708 Admiral Forbin, with a naval force transporting the Old Pretender and 6000 troops, attempted a landing in Scotland but on reaching the Firth of Forth was forced to return to Dunkirk. In 1719 a Spanish army of some 6000 under the Jacobite Duke of Ormonde intended to land in the west of England. A diversionary force commanded by Scotland's Earl Marischal, George Keith, was to head for Scotland to raise the clans. In the event, only the diversionary force escaped the storms which forced the main body to return to La Coruña. Keith's 1000 men landed but were not supported and were crushed at Glen Shiel.

The next attempt was to be a surprise attack with 10,000 men under the Comte de Saxe in January 1744 at a time when the prevailing winds would be easterly – which would prevent the English fleet at Portsmouth from coming out of Spithead, or it might be drawn away to the west leaving the south-east coast unprotected. Saxe would then sail from Dunkirk and land at Maldon, Essex. The scheme failed through delays, counter-intelligence and, finally, destructive storms.

The following year was critical. A French attack on the south coast to synchronize with Charles Edward's Jacobite invasion from Scotland might have been disastrous for George II. Preparations were openly made at Dunkirk for a landing in the Blackwater or in the Thames Estuary but the real invasion force was to gather in the Calais/Boulogne area. With the navy expecting a threat to the east coast, the Dunkirk fleet would sail west instead, embark the troops

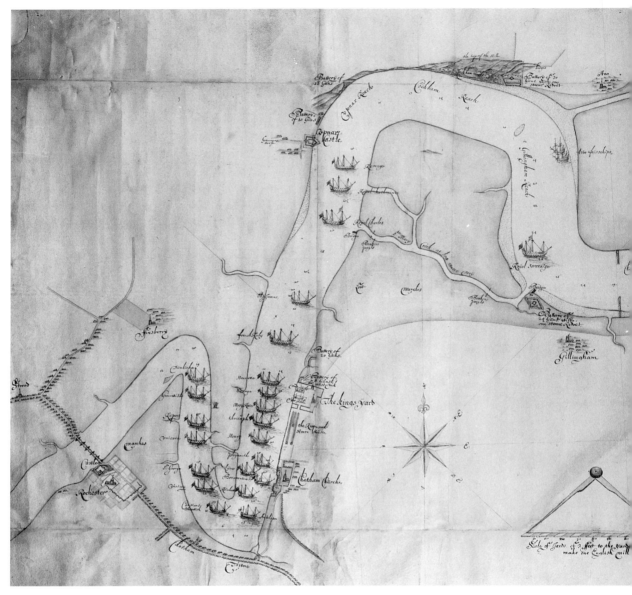

5 *The river at Chatham with the new batteries and the fleet at anchor by Sir Bernard de Gomme, 1669.*

at Boulogne, and put them ashore in the neighbourhood of Rye in Sussex. There was, however, no concerted action between the Jacobites and the French. The crew of a captured French transport ship revealed the tactics to be used and surprise was lost.

The Seven Years War led to a renewal of French invasion schemes. In 1756, 50,000 troops were assembled for a landing dependent on a diversionary attack on the British base of Port Mahon, Minorca. However, though Minorca was lost, the Channel Fleet remained in position and the invasion attempt had to be postponed. The plan was revived in 1759 on a more elaborate scale and threats and rumours of invasion persisted in England month after month. The fatal flaw, like the 1588 Armada before it, was the geographical separation of the enemy land and naval forces. The eventual decisive battle in Quiberon Bay destroyed

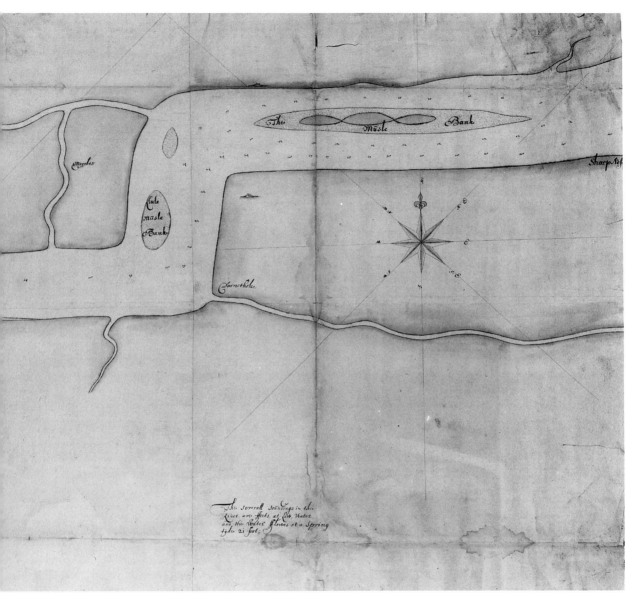

the French navy as a fighting force and all expectations of invasion of Britain had to be abandoned. Yet the diversionary attempt by Thurot on northern Ireland did get through and the town and castle of Carrickfergus were briefly captured.

Despite the disaster of Quiberon Bay, French invasion schemes intensified and Choiseul, now in alliance with Spain, looked towards a colonial diversion. A siege of Gibraltar would occupy the Mediterranean fleet and a French fleet would be sent to the Caribbean to draw off Admiral Rodney. A new French squadron was to be assembled at Ferrol to give the illusion that it was intended for Gibraltar. A force of 50,000 troops would then be diverted to the Channel coast, and with the element of surprise, a beachhead would be established. The real intentions of the French were discovered and with Ferrol now blockaded, the attempt of 1762 came to nothing.

Three years later, the Comte de Broglie submitted a comprehensive invasion project. With six overseas diversionary operations which would lure away the Royal Navy, a French army of 60,000 men in four divisions would be landed at Rye, Winchelsea, Hastings and Pevensey. Choiseul strengthened the scheme by recognizing that a naval battle was a prerequisite to any credible invasion project. Further thinking suggested a beachhead between Littlehampton and Chichester with Portsmouth and the Isle of Wight as an immediate objective.

The best opportunity for French success came while Britain was involved in North America. In 1779, Britain was at her most isolated and open to what has been called the 'other Armada' of Franco-Spanish co-operation. A series of diversionary attacks were necessary to achieve local superiority in the Channel. The objective focused on Portsmouth with the idea of retaining it as a French Gibraltar. This objective was modified by Dumouriez, who proposed that the Isle of Wight, not Portsmouth, should serve as the French Gibraltar thus depriving Britain of its greatest dockyard. It was thought that the numerical superiority of the Franco-Spanish fleet in the Channel would achieve victory especially as many British ships were engaged in America. A force of 20,000 infantry based in Normandy would then proceed against Portsmouth. The French commander was to consider Plymouth as his secondary objective. The French launched a diversionary raid on the Channel Islands and the British government could not be sure where the main invasion thrust would fall. The attempt of 1779 ended in fiasco, however, due to a lack of co-operation on the part of the allies, with delays and incompetence leading to sickness and shortage of provisions, so that despite the fleet having come within sight of Plymouth, neither side brought the other to battle, and the French fleet was eventually forced to retire to Brest.

The political impact of the French Revolution caused the traditional Anglo-French rivalry to take on fresh impetus and the drafting of invasion schemes continued as a French pastime. In 1793 preparations were made for an invasion but the fleet at Brest was in no state to put to sea. General Lazare Hoche was among the most enthusiastic advocates of invasion. 'Ever since the beginning of the war I have never ceased to believe that it is in their own country that we must attack the English.' He believed that it would be possible with quite small numbers to conduct destructive raiding parties which would attempt to rally the politically disaffected and generate sabotage and guerilla activity. The West Country was to be the first objective but then the possibility of the capture of Ireland seemed much more propitious under the promptings of Wolfe Tone, the Irish revolutionary leader.

In December 1796 the last great invasion force to sail for the British Isles set out. Altogether there were nearly 15,000 men in 45 ships which arrived in Bantry Bay but without the frigate carrying Hoche himself. The French waited for him to arrive before disembarking and were then caught in a violent storm which effectively ended the attempt. This episode, however, was proof that the British fleet was not infallible. The Western Squadron stationed at Spithead was too far up-Channel to deal with this French force approaching Ireland, and the cruising squadrons and the frigates covering Brest had been eluded. In 1797 the disruption caused by the naval mutinies at Spithead and the Nore enabled the assembly of 13,500 Dutch troops off Texel with Scotland as their objective. Only by meeting the mutineers' demands could Admiral Duncan's fleet sail out and defeat the Dutch off Camperdown.

In line with Hoche's policy, an Irish–American, Colonel Tate, intended to land near Bristol and spread a terrorist campaign as a diversion for the Irish landing. Because of British warships in the Bristol Channel, Tate and his 1200-strong 'Black Legion', largely obtained from French gaols, were put ashore at Fishguard – the last invasion of Britain. It lasted three days.

A new 'army of England' was formed the next year to be put ashore from specially constructed gunboats and fishing boats. However, Napoleon Bonaparte was now in power and was convinced that a successful operation could only be achieved following a major French victory at sea.

The great Irish rebellion of 1798 invited French participation but, by the time General

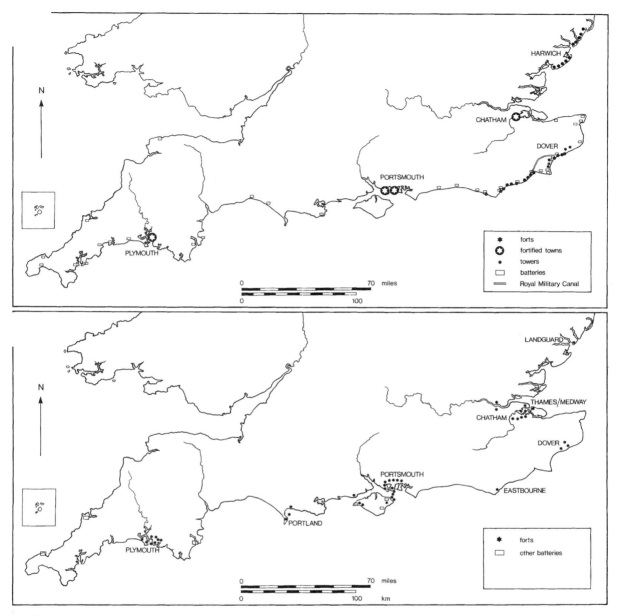

6 (i) *Concentrations of defences during the Napoleonic Wars.*
(ii) *Mid-nineteenth-century fortification programme.*

Humbert had landed with a small force at Killala Bay, the uprising had been crushed. A second expedition came to nothing. Intended to synchronize with Humbert's landing, a force of 3000 men succeeded in reaching Lough Swilly only to be defeated decisively by a naval force. Despite a victory at Castlebar, Humbert's cause was lost at Ballinamuck, but following his release he continued to advocate the seizure of Ireland together with terrorist and sabotage raids on England by criminals released from French gaols.

More formidable were the preparations organized in 1801 by Napoleon and centred on Boulogne. These invasion preparations were more in the way of a rehearsal for a scheme which was to dominate the years 1803–5 (**6**). The new enterprise was for two huge flotillas, one at

7 *'The great Raft, now building at Brest.' An English cartoon of c. 1798 purporting to show a monster raft designed for transporting whole regiments of French troops in an invasion attempt.*

Dunkirk, the other at Cherbourg, with specially designed gunboats and transports (**7**). All the embarkation ports had been improved and vast camps for something in the region of 100,000 men established. Preparations continued during 1804. In Napoleon's view it only required mastery of the Straits for six hours to obtain his bridgehead 'and we shall be masters of the world'. By then he had abandoned the idea of using fog or winter's darkness to evade the British warships. Command of the Channel had to be achieved however temporarily. Ireland again suggested itself as a diversion. Admiral Ganteaume was asked to land 16,000 troops sailing from Brest to Lough Swilly. The French fleet from Toulon was sent to the West Indies to draw off the Royal Navy and the tactic partially

worked. Yet the timidity and incompetence of Villeneuve in failing to take advantage of a situation when there were only seventeen British ships to dispute the Western Approaches was the cause of its failure. Once the initiative had been lost, Napoleon accepted that the chance of an invasion had gone. His only alternative means of weakening Britain was by economic blockade.

Nineteenth-century invasion scares and panics
The great naval victories of the Napoleonic Wars might be thought to have produced a state of confidence in Britain's national security during the nineteenth century, yet a popular nervousness continued. Memories of Napoleon's army across the Channel remained vivid and the perceived viciousness of the French meant that chances could not be taken. Anxieties were not eased by the publication in France of pamphlets analysing the effectiveness of British coastal defences and speculating how Britain could be successfully invaded. There were always Frenchmen who

would publicly devise schemes to diminish British imperial power. Such provocations did not lessen as the century advanced; but as the reality of invasion became more remote so there was closer public scrutiny of the country's defensive capabilities. Were the coastal fortifications up to date? Were the ships as advanced as those of Britain's rivals and in sufficiently overwhelming numbers?

The feeling of insecurity was not entirely irrational. The rifled-gun and especially the emergence of steam-powered ironclad ships in mid-century had revolutionized warfare. The changing nature of artillery, explosives and armour was now universally apparent through reports in newspapers and the illustrated popular magazines. By the turn of the twentieth century, the rise of German naval power only served to emphasize Britain's vulnerability.

These latent fears were first seriously aroused in 1847 by the 'leaking' to the *Morning Chronicle* of a letter from the Duke of Wellington to Sir John Burgoyne, Inspector General of Fortifications, in which he expressed the view that the application of steam-power to warships facilitated invasion. The English Channel was no longer the obstacle it had been to the sailing ship. Indeed, two years earlier, Lord Palmerston expressed the point effectively when he told the House of Commons that 'Steam navigation has rendered that which was before impassable by a military force nothing more than a river passable by a steam bridge.' In 1846 General Sir John Burgoyne had drawn up a lengthy paper entitled 'Observations on the Possible Results of a War with France under our Present System of Military Preparation'. The paper repeated the long-standing argument that the French might obtain temporary naval superiority in the Channel long enough to stage an invasion in great force and, given the current level of military capability and preparedness, he concluded that they would probably succeed. Pressure on the government became intense and income tax had to be almost doubled to meet limited military requirements. The 'panic' quickly evaporated when, early in 1848, Louis Philippe fled to England to escape the revolutionaries in Paris.

The second 'panic' occurred in 1851–2 caused by the *coup d'état* of Louis Napoleon and his subsequent election as Emperor. Palmerston was again the leading scaremonger. He insisted that 50,000 or 60,000 French troops could be secretly transported from Cherbourg and put ashore in a single night. It was demonstrated, however, that this could not possibly be achieved without a substantial and very visible build-up of naval force; but, despite this artificial invasion scare, it had the effect of stimulating a programme of fortification construction which included the Solent and the Channel Islands.

The third 'panic' was essentially due to French involvement in naval technological progress. There was also undoubted suspicion and fear of the personal motives and ambitions of Napoleon III. Military success in Italy was dangerous enough but the rapid construction of ironclads and rifled guns and the commencement of the Suez Canal all appeared to be demonstrably anti-British. In 1859 the armoured steam frigate *La Gloire* was launched – to British consternation. Rumours of troop concentrations at the newly enlarged and fortified harbour of Cherbourg encouraged belief in the imminent threat of invasion, not only in the popular mind but also at the War Office. A Royal Commission on the Defences of the United Kingdom was set up, publishing its report early in 1860 (see **6**).

Even after the greatest fortress building programme that Britain had ever witnessed, as a result of the Royal Commission's recommendations, there were still uncertainties. *Blackwoods* magazine in 1871 published a short story, *The Battle of Dorking Gap*, by a Royal Engineer officer, Lieutenant-Colonel Sir George Chesney, whose plot focused on a successful German invasion of England. The invasion was possible because Chesney had invoked the time-old justification for land defences – the temporary absence of the fleet. Chesney's real objective was to encourage the Volunteer Movement and greater preparedness in home defence. He provided further support for the widely held view that defence against invasion was ultimately the responsibility of the regular and auxiliary troops and the fixed defences along the coast.

In 1886 the military claimed that the coastal defences were again inadequate and drew attention to the surprising fact that London itself was unprotected. An article in the *Daily Telegraph* in 1888, inspired by comments by Field Marshal von Moltke, gave credence to this belief by stating that the French could land by surprise some 20,000 to 30,000 men between Dover and Portsmouth. In face of conflicting advice and despite the earlier invasion panic, the Naval Defence Act of 1889 showed that the 'Blue Water School' had in fact won the debate and resources were predominantly put into new warships.

Invasion was not the only threat causing alarm during the 1880s. The possibility of destructive raids by hostile cruisers and torpedo boats on commercial ports and shipping produced its own response (**8**). It led to the appointment of a parliamentary committee in 1882 to enquire into the defences of the mercantile ports; its report was to be nearly as significant as the Royal Commission on National Defences of 1859.

In 1891 Edward Stanhope, Secretary of State for War, laid down the doctrine that the primary duty of the army was home defence: the employment of even an army corps in the field in a European war was stated to be improbable. By 1893–4, another naval 'scare' led to the construction of the *Royal Sovereign* class of battleship but there was also greater recognition of the need to defend a wider range of mercantile ports. With the turn of the twentieth century home defence came to occupy a major place in military thinking and collaboration between the War Office and the Admiralty at last culminated in the creation of the Committee of Imperial Defence. There was accompanying public concern. William Le Queux's novel *The Invasion of 1910* was serialised in the *Daily Mail* in 1908 and Guy du Maurier's play *An Englishman's Home* (1909) was a dramatized account of an invasion; these were only part of a popular literature on the subject.

At the time of Haldane's reorganization of the army in 1907, there was pressure for conscription to match the practice of Britain's continental rivals. Sir Ian Hamilton's book *Compulsory Service* (1911) argued strongly against it, stressing the advantages of a voluntary professional army and the organization of a part-time Territorial Force for home defence. The tradition of the militia and volunteer movement was revived to be continued somewhat later as the Local Defence Volunteers and the Home Guard of 1940, which undertook the manning of many defence positions.

Out of this atmosphere in Edwardian Britain came three inquiries (1903, 1907 and 1914) into the likelihood of invasion. The first produced a

8 *'Just completed at Toulon', a French torpedo boat of the 1890s.*

report which generated the belief that an invasion could not be launched successfully with a force of less than 70,000 men which would require 200 boats and at least twenty hours to disembark. The second inquiry confirmed the 'Blue Water' approach to the extent that the committee thought that land defences were now redundant. On the eve of the war, however, the annual naval manoeuvres of 1912 and 1913 demonstrated that the 'enemy' fleet evaded detection long enough for it to be possible to throw on to the east coast forces of between 12,000 and 48,000 men. In April 1914 a report entitled 'Attack on the British Isles from Overseas' recommended increases in the defences of the Humber, Tyne and Harwich.

Twentieth-century threats

Fear of invasion therefore remained a constant concern for British strategists and continued during the First World War; although with hindsight its likelihood then was remote given the military stalemate on the Western Front. Still, hostile occupation of the Flemish coast was always held to offer a springboard for such an attack and there was always the possibility that the navy could be drawn out of position.

More significantly came new dimensions to warfare which were to intensify as the twentieth century moved on and brought the civilian population directly into the conflict. The first was air-power and bombing. Warnings of attacks needed to be given, public shelters provided as well as individual protection and civil defence instituted. After the use of poison gas on the Western Front and later by the Italians in Abyssinia, civilians were clearly at risk. Traditional dangers intensified. Vastly more effective forms of blockade and the threat of national starvation were posed by widespread use of sea mines and submarines. The pattern of warfare had changed so much that a line has to be drawn between the twentieth century and what had existed during the previous four centuries. The whole conception of defence planning altered just as it was to change fundamentally after the development of the atomic bomb of 1945.

After 1918 came demobilization, but 'fixed' coast defences were maintained to a degree. Their armament, however, was on the verge of obsolescence. As for air defence, 'by the end of 1920 not a gun or a searchlight was deployed for the protection of London and not one fighter squadron was specifically assigned to home defence'. The first post-war Coalition Government had made an assumption that there would be no major war involving the British empire for the next ten years. This 'ten-year rule' was to govern defence considerations until 1932 when political developments in Germany began to give concern, and rearmament began in earnest in 1936. In the meantime, keeping up with the traditional enemy, France, was the spur to improving the air force.

The probability of invasion during the summer and autumn of 1940 was in everyone's minds. Hitler's Operation 'Sealion' has since been closely scrutinized and established as a genuine threat (**9**).

In May the Home Defence Executive was set up to supervise a drastic overhaul of British defence measures. Emphasis was given to protection against airborne forces and infantry were allotted to ports and their fixed defences. The most vulnerable area for projected seaborne landings, supported by air-power, particularly dive-bombers, was the stretch of coast from Sussex to the Wash. Various schemes were prepared for denying ports to the enemy by means of blockships, mines and demolition charges. The Local Defence Volunteers (LDV), the predecessors of the Home Guard, were formed. Local seaward defences of estuaries and harbours were not thought proof against light surface craft as the navy had not nearly enough destroyers or patrol vessels to cover the whole coast. On the eve of the Dunkirk evacuation, therefore, the whole Home forces were neither equipped nor trained to deal with an enemy well supplied with armour. Because of the lack of suitable transport, troops could only expect hired motor coaches in order to achieve any kind of mobility.

The decision to withdraw British forces from the isolated position at Dunkirk was made on

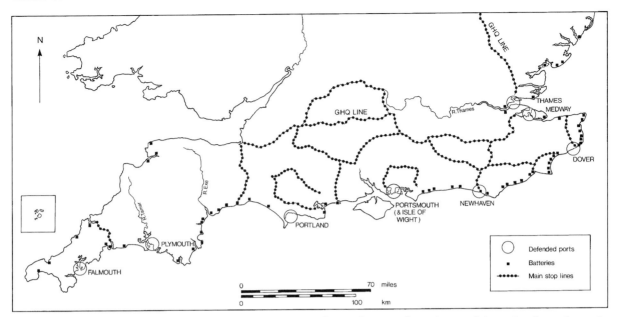

9 *Map of the defences of southern England in 1940 show-ing the defended ports, emergency batteries and the principal stop-lines.*

26 May 1940, and the evacuation ended on 4 June. German invasion now seemed probable; a situation made more daunting by the army's loss of all its heavy weapons and equipment in France. By the third week in June about 150,000 civilians besides troops were engaged on defences.

Hitler's order for Operation 'Sealion' was not issued until 16 July but the idea of invasion first received his attention on 21 May. The Inter-Service Committee on Invasion anticipated a frontal attack through Kent and Sussex. Indeed, the revised Operation 'Sealion' plan of September 1940 showed landing areas between Brighton and Folkestone. Invasion barges and landing craft were assembled in credible numbers along the French and Belgian coasts. Command of the air, however, was the prerequisite for any success and the German Admiralty was never sanguine about the prospects of a successful landing. The right combination of circumstances, together with the German failure to eliminate the Royal Air Force, meant that once more invasion did not materialize.

2
The role of the navy

The naval historian Stephen Roskill wrote: 'The foundation of maritime power is to win and keep control of the seas for one's own use, and to deny such control to one's adversaries.' The second function of sea-power is to give security against invasion. This chapter is no place to attempt a thumbnail historical review of the Royal Navy but it is necessary to consider its part in protecting the country and the defensive strategies it adopted at various times. It was after all the first line of defence until the arrival of air-power, and there were those who claimed that it was the only defence needed to prevent invasion.

There are several underlying factors which govern thinking about the defence of the Channel coasts. In the first place is the importance of the prevailing south-west wind; a considerable concern to both attacker and defender in the age of sail. The proximity of the European mainland opposite Dover and south-east Kent concentrated minds as well as the shipping lanes. J.A. Williamson described the English coast as easier to navigate than the French with fewer outlying dangers, and wrote that its tides are comparatively simple to work. The French coast abounds in reefs and sands lying well out and the tides are fiercer and subject to marked local variations. At all times, therefore, shipping has tended to follow the English coasts. Before the days of artificial harbours, the north French coast was deficient in ports for the greater ships of war and there was a shortage of suitable places from which an invasion of Britain might be mounted. By contrast, British coasts had a number of suitable harbours. British naval bases for the defence of the Channel since the sixteenth century have been Plymouth, Portsmouth and Chatham, supplemented by anchorages at Torbay, the Downs and the Nore, and later by the harbours of refuge: Ramsgate, Portland and Dover (**10**).

The medieval background

Anglo Saxon and medieval kings used merchant ships which could be adapted for warfare for coastal defence but there was no navy on a permanent basis. The maritime crisis for the English crown in 1204, due to the loss of Normandy, caused King John to develop a fleet of galleys divided into four squadrons for the east coast, south-east, south and south-west. Some were based on Southampton, and Portsmouth Harbour developed as a putative fleet base.

The organization of south-eastern ports known as the Cinque Ports (Dover, Sandwich, Romney, Hythe and Hastings etc.) was sufficiently effective for kings to treat its ships as a naval resource in an emergency. The ports were granted the profits of some of their courts in return for 15 days' sea-service of 57 ships a year. The Cinque Ports were particularly significant during the thirteenth century. The ports of Dover, Winchelsea, Sandwich, Rye and others had, however, no defence against the natural shifts of sand and mud which silted their harbours. During the course of the later Middle Ages their effectiveness as an organization declined.

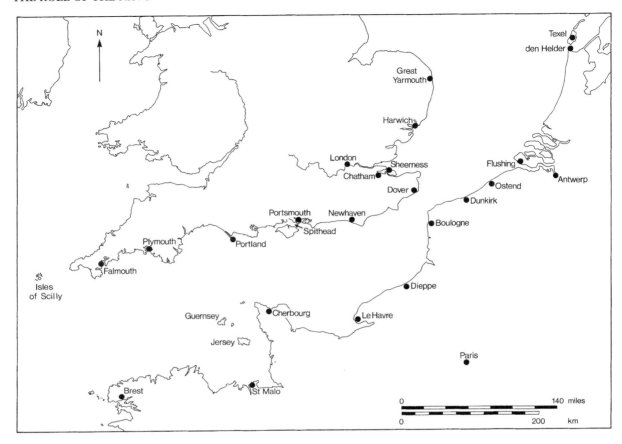

10 *Map of the English Channel from Brest to Texel, indicating the main ports and naval bases.*

The Hundred Years War (c. 1330–c. 1450) saw the beginnings of national identity in warfare. Cross-Channel raiding became more organized and frequent. French raids on southern coastal towns are well documented. The royal war fleet too became more and more a regular feature. The earliest surviving list of ships owned by the king was compiled in 1417. Continuity in keeping up a royal fleet was lacking and stimulated the political polemic, *The Libelle of English Polycye*, which was published in 1436 to rouse the government of the day from apathy and, among other things, to clear the Channel of pirates and maintain safe communications with Calais: 'Cheryshe marchandyse, kepe thamyralte [the admiralty], That we bee maysteres of the narrowe see.'

Royal ships were built in the Thames at Greenwich and Southampton Water, and a forge and storehouse were established temporarily at Southampton. The main anchorage of the king's great ships in the fifteenth century was the Hamble, its entrance fortified by a bulwark or tower and spiked pales. The lowest part of the hull of the *Grace Dieu*, built in 1418, still lies there in the mud. There are lists of the royal ships that show a variety of vessels, which were mostly merchantmen in their primary function, but there were those which were clearly warships divided into squadrons. Their purpose was to protect the coasts, escort convoys of merchantmen and transport military forces and supplies across the Channel.

Tudor strategy

The maritime policy of the early Tudors was concentrated upon preserving supremacy in the

Channel rather than attacking foreign convoys or challenging the overseas territorial claims of Spain and Portugal. 'The Tudor fleet was basically a water-borne home defence squadron.'

The establishing of a permanent Royal Navy, however, should be credited to the Tudor monarchy. Henry VIII inherited a small fleet of seven ships in 1509. His father's construction of a dry dock at Portsmouth was of fundamental importance and underlined the need to fortify the town and the entrance to Portsmouth Harbour. Portsmouth was the best base for a fleet intended to command the eastern Channel. The fleet operated between Brest and the Thames Estuary but was commissioned only for the summer. In 1545 the French had designs on Portsmouth, anchoring off Ryde and St Helens and landing on the Isle of Wight. It was on this occasion that the royal flagship, *Mary Rose*, was lost through faulty seamanship (see **3**). Because of Portsmouth's apparent vulnerability at the time, Henry withdrew shipbuilding activity from there, and the laying up of the royal fleet when out of commission was established on the Thames at Deptford and Woolwich.

The emergence of English sea-power in the sixteenth century coincided with technical improvements in gunnery and development of ship design. It was Henry VIII who created a battle fleet which began to exploit the use of guns on a scale which took the warship outside the medieval custom of close-quarter fighting. The mounting of the main armament along the sides of the ship and on several decks led to the development of broadside gunfire familiar to the ships of Nelson's navy. Maintaining a full-time fleet, nevertheless, was still a problem and the loss of Calais was partly attributed to the lack of a naval force in the Straits of Dover.

The Elizabethan navy was also organized primarily for coastal defence but this role began to be widened following the 1588 Armada crisis. At the beginning of Elizabeth's reign, the navy had an eastern emphasis with its fleet based at Chatham, protected by the purpose-built Upnor Castle (see **4**). This made sense while political and military concerns centred on the Spanish Netherlands. The long-standing dictum that the Scheldt Estuary is 'a pistol pointed at the heart of England' meant that English military support for the Dutch Protestants entailed action in Zeeland and at Flushing.

When the Spanish invasion threat materialized in 1588, the prevailing south-westerly winds were to Spanish advantage and dictated English counter-measures. The division of the English ships at the time was roughly 50 in the Downs anchorage, between Deal and Walmer and the Goodwin Sands, and 102 at Plymouth. It was crucial to get the fleet to windward of the Spanish ships and follow their progress up-Channel, snapping at the flanks of the great crescent formation of the Armada until, having anchored off Gravelines, the Spaniards were dispersed by the use of fireships (see **colour plate** 3).

The value of Drake's policy for pre-emptive strikes on invasion preparations, and the attack on the Armada while still in Cadiz Harbour, had wider implications on defensive policies. The next year, John Hawkins attempted to define a wider strategy which went beyond the fleet's duty to 'ply up and down in the chops of the Channel'. Hawkins, though primarily for financial gain, was among the first advocates of what was later to be known as the 'Blue Water School' as he pressed for a forward and aggressive policy of meeting Spanish naval-power and the treasure fleets far out in the Western Approaches. In particular, he proposed the blockading of the Azores while the remainder of the queen's ships were to be kept in home waters to secure the Channel. Eventually the greater part of the Elizabethan navy was transformed from a short-range, Narrow Seas fleet, which was essentially a coastal defence operation, into a high-seas fleet capable of operating at long range as an ocean going force as well.

Anglo-Dutch naval wars

Under the early Stuart kings the navy declined as a defensive force. English coastal waters were prey to privateers chiefly from Dunkirk and even from Barbary corsairs from North Africa. The degree to which the navy had lost command of the Narrow Seas was demonstrated in 1639 when a Spanish fleet bound for Antwerp took refuge in the Downs and was there overwhelmed by a Dutch fleet under Admiral van Tromp.

It was therefore somewhat ironic that, at a time of naval weakness of will, a proprietorial attitude was adopted over the surrounding seas. The claim to the sovereignty of the so-called 'British Seas' extending from Norway to Cape Finisterre was expressed by John Seldon in *Mare Clausum Seu Dominicium Maris* of 1635, a revival and redefining of a vague and ancient claim of English kings. The concept was taken up by the Commonwealth and equally by the restored monarchy of 1660. The 'Channel Salute' (the demand that foreign vessels should strike their topsails and take in their flags when meeting an English warship in the 'British Seas') was indeed the catalyst for the First Dutch War. To the Dutch, freedom of navigation was a firm principle, and they were unimpressed by such claims.

The navy developed after the Civil War and as early as 1650 Captain William Penn, Commander-in-Chief, was charged with guarding the Channel from Beachy Head to Lands End with six ships. This system continued following the Restoration. It was the start of what was to become a Western Squadron with a brief to harry Dutch seaborne trade as well as to maintain a defensive role. The main naval actions of the Dutch wars, however, were, apart from the battle off Portland in 1663, almost entirely off the eastern coasts. Lack of sufficient finance to keep the Royal Navy on a more than seasonal basis was its undoing. The inability to maintain the fleet in commission led to the disastrous Dutch raid on the Medway in 1667 (**colour plate 4**).

Greater use was now being made of Plymouth as a base but it lacked proper repair or victualling provision. In France, on the other hand, naval development under Colbert in the 1670s saw the revival of the dockyards at Toulon, Rochefort, Brest, Le Havre and Dunkirk, with the construction of a fleet of warships which were more numerous, larger, more heavily armed and better designed than the English.

A most important lesson in the vulnerability of the Channel coast was learnt in 1688 when William of Orange demonstrated that it was possible to effect a successful 'invasion' of England despite the presence of a vastly superior home fleet. It was an east wind which kept Lord Dartmouth's ships in the Thames, allowing William to elude the Royal Navy and make a landing at Torbay with his small army. How far there was the political will on the part of Dartmouth to prevent this result is a matter of conjecture but the event remained an example to the 'Bolt from the Blue School' that the navy was not infallible and circumstances could allow a successful invasion.

Two years later, Tourville gained complete command of the Narrow Seas for the French fleet. Nevertheless, after the Battle of Beachy Head in 1690, when the English fleet was chased up the Channel by Tourville and driven to take refuge in the Thames, Admiral Torrington wrote:

Most men were in fear that the French would invade but I was always of another opinion, for I always said that, whilst we had a fleet in being, they would not dare to make an attempt.

The principle of the 'fleet in being' meant that no admiral would undertake an invasion of Britain unless he had very great superiority of naval force.

The course of the war, however, changed following the significant French defeat at Barfleur–La Hogue, Normandy, in 1692. From then on the main area of British naval activity moved westward.

Under Queen Anne naval strategy changed and became more aggressive. The main fleet was intended primarily for offensive purposes with sometimes a few first- and second-rates kept as a reserve at home. After the expedition to Toulon in 1707, the Main Fleet changed character. Its objectives moved towards trade protection. The English cruising squadrons were now divided into two. The North Sea (the Downs or Dunkirk) Squadron had bases at Harwich, Deal and Dover and three principal rendezvous: the Downs, off

Deal and Sandwich; Hollesley Bay, Suffolk; and Yarmouth Roads, Norfolk. The Channel Soundings Squadron was based on Plymouth and its new dockyard, sheltering in Torbay and Scilly. Measures had to be taken against privateers operating from Brest to St Malo and this called for the stationing of small craft around the coast and the employment of larger warships to escort convoys up and down the Channel. In 1708 the Cruizers and Convoy Act provided the foundation of commerce protection as well as of international prize law.

The Western Squadron
The eighteenth century saw the fitful rise in the ascendancy of the Royal Navy. The increase in colonial acquisitions meant that its preoccupations were far flung: in the Mediterranean, West Indies and the Americas and Indian Ocean. By threatening an invasion of Britain, therefore, France could limit British impact in the wider sphere by tying down powerful British squadrons to guard against an attack which might never come. Alternatively, if serious invasion was planned, France could use diversionary tactics in Britain's widespread colonies in order to draw the Royal Navy out of the Channel. In contrast, the 'Blue Water' strategy required that Britain in wartime should decline continental commitments and confine itself to naval operations, which it was believed would be sufficient to defend the country against invasion and defeat the enemy by blockade and commerce raiding. Blockade was the corner-stone of British strategy, though close blockade was established relatively late. It had been attempted in the Dutch wars and used against Brest in 1690 but it was never applied effectively until the Seven Years War (1756–63).

In the 'crisis year' of 1745, a French invasion was expected to take advantage of the Jacobite Highland rebellion. A strong squadron was assembled in the Downs under Admiral Vernon. Yet the major strategic development was the establishment of the Western Squadron in 'the Soundings' (the Western Approaches). Naval historians have recently pointed out that the idea of

guarding the English Channel by keeping the main fleet out to windward in the Western Approaches was not a new one. Something like it had been adopted in 1588 on the advice of Sir Francis Drake but it was now for the first time clearly articulated and developed. Neither France at that date nor Spain had a naval base in the Channel proper so any enemy fleet had to come from westward. A large proportion of French naval strength was based on Brest and Rochfort. An invasion force might sail from the ports of Normandy and Brittany but it would sail without naval escort unless a fleet came up the Channel to cover it. Most of Britain's foreign trade at this time, except with the Baltic, came up and down the Channel. If the main fleet cruised to the westward it was well placed to cover convoys outward and homeward bound; it could watch the main French naval base of Brest and intercept fleets coming and going from it, guard against any attempt to invade Ireland and oppose an enemy fleet entering the Channel. In developing this principle, Vernon was one of the most important theorists, and Anson, as Commander-in-Chief of the Western Squadron for most of 1746 and 1747, was an active practitioner. The Western or Channel Squadron formed the core of Britain's naval strategy for a century or more. It was not primarily a defence against invasion but a means of commanding the sea.

Close blockade of Brest was undertaken to prevent invasion threats in 1759, 1801 and 1803–5. At other times a loose blockade was maintained by a squadron making a series of sweeps into the Bay of Biscay during the summer, withdrawing to Torbay for revictualling, while frigates off Brest watched French movements. In winter the squadron stayed moored in Torbay or Spithead leaving the frigates to continue their watch. The choice of home port – Plymouth or Portsmouth – for the Western Squadron was controversial. Spithead, or the anchorage of St Helens, was convenient but too far up-Channel; Torbay was dangerously exposed either to enemy attack or to a south-easterly wind; Cawsand Bay, to the west of Plymouth, was a cramped and exposed anchorage, while the Hamoaze at the mouth of the Tamar took far too long to get in or out of. Vernon argued for keeping the main Western Squadron at sea 'in Soundings', with a force of smaller ships to guard the Narrow Seas against invasion. Anson agreed but favoured keeping the main force in port until the enemy was known to be preparing to put to sea and not risking dispersal until he had been met and defeated.

At the same time the eastern coasts were not neglected. In 1752 Sir Isaac Townshend, Admiral of the Blue, hoisted his flag at the buoy of the Nore and created the Nore Command. This included the Downs, the lesser anchorages of Harwich and Yarmouth, and all the sea approaches to London. The Nore – the meeting-place of the Thames and Medway – was the chief rendezvous of the navy throughout the days of sail. In 1759 one group of ships kept watch on Dunkirk and the Flemish ports, a second lay in the Downs, and a third at Spithead covering Portsmouth and watching Le Havre. Vernon had earlier established an intelligence and early-warning system using sloops, cutters and small yachts in the Channel manned by volunteers.

By the end of the Seven Years War the navy had grown considerably but, with the exception of Plymouth and Portsmouth, its dockyards had remained virtually unaltered since the sixteenth and seventeenth centuries when the navy's responsibilities were concentrated to eastward. Four of the six major yards were situated there. Only Plymouth was well placed to support the Western Squadron as it developed as the centre-piece of British naval strategy. Woolwich, Deptford and Sheerness all suffered from cramped sites which inhibited expansion; the Medway at Chatham was shoaling badly and Sheerness, which at least had easy access to the open sea, was affected by malaria and shipworm. The Western Squadron's supplies had to come up far to leeward. There was a victualling crisis in 1758 when the Western Squadron under Hawke first attempted the blockade of Brest and the ships could not be satisfactorily maintained. This was a general problem which was eased, as

far as the Plymouth-based ships were concerned, by the building in the next century of the extensive Royal William Victualling Yard at Stonehouse.

For some time it had become an established feature of British naval policy in peacetime to maintain a force of 'guardships', or warships in commission in port though not completely ready for sea. In theory they were there to guard the dockyard ports from any sudden attack and act as a reserve, but in Nicholas Rogers' view their real function was to make up Britain's acknowledged weakness in mobilizing manpower for the navy. Every man mustered aboard a guardship was one less to recruit on the approach of hostilities, and the guardships might form a squadron ready for immediate use on the outbreak of war. Since the guardships were the only means of mobilizing a squadron quickly, they were the principal naval deterrent.

In 1776 France and Spain had more ships in commission in the European sphere of operations than Britain. Then in 1779 there came the 'Other Armada', the most formidable invasion threat that the country had faced since 1588 (described in the previous chapter). There was a shortage of frigates for home defence since most were in American waters during the course of the War of American Independence. This degree of dispersal created, in some respects, the worst crisis in the navy's history and when Britain came nearest to defeat at sea. In 1781 another Combined Fleet sailed into the Channel and the North Sea also became a theatre of war requiring ships to blockade Texel. The Western Squadron was in effect abandoned except for a force of about twenty fast ships of the line in the hope of making any invasion scheme impossibly difficult.

By the time of the French Revolutionary and Napoleonic Wars it was the view of Admirals St Vincent and Nelson that the first line of defence was on the enemy's coast. Open blockade was adopted by Howe, a matter merely of observation, with the fleet remaining at Spithead. Close blockade was re-established by St Vincent with Brest the most important blockade station, again neutralizing the main French fleet base. As was proved, however, by events in Ireland and Pembrokeshire, it was always possible for an enemy to fling ashore a small force so that an effective degree of maritime control was an essential preliminary to check a serious invasion.

Naval forces during the invasion threat of 1803–15 were divided between the North Sea Fleet and the Western Squadron or Channel Fleet, as it was also known, whose eastern limit was Selsey Bill, and with squadrons at Plymouth, Channel Islands and Portsmouth. By 1803, Admiral Lord Keith was in command of the North Sea Fleet whose responsibilities extended from Selsey Bill to Scotland with his headquarters at Ramsgate, where the harbour of refuge had recently been completed. Within the North Sea Fleet was the Downs Squadron, intended to protect the entrance to the Channel, with the Dungeness Squadron watching Boulogne and other Channel ports which were used to assemble the landing vessels. The Downs Squadron became the central element of the anti-invasion forces. Other Squadrons were at the Nore and Yarmouth. Lord Keith declared:

> I have ever held a squadron of stout ships in the Downs to be of essential consequence, because I can hardly believe that the French troops will ever embark unless covered by a squadron proceeding into the Channel, either straight up or north about; both are difficult and dangerous but not impracticable.

The ships were mostly frigates and sloops but also included smaller 'gun-brigs' intended to work inshore against the invasion craft (**11**).

Keith was also responsible for organizing the Sea Fencibles, the chain of coast signal stations and the shutter telegraph to London, the extension of the chain of Martello towers and general liaison with the army (**12**). The Sea Fencibles had been established as volunteers for the defence of the coast, to be instructed 'in the use of cannon and pikes'. Among their duties was the manning

11 *'The Trinity Flotilla' at the Hope near Gravesend in Line of Battle; 1804* (European Magazine).

12 *Coastal signal station, an example of those established in Sussex, 1794–1814. In the house lived a naval lieutenant, a midshipman and two seamen. Two soldiers were housed nearby to take urgent messages to the local army commander.*

of the Martello towers, help with the chain of signal stations as well as operating their own boats to supplement the regular warships.

As part of the Channel Fleet were the Irish and Channel Islands or Guernsey squadrons. These were quite small and served to prevent a French invasion of those islands, to check the St Malo privateers and to provide intelligence. In 1812 they had twelve ships. The Western Squadron's long-term strategy, however, was eventually undermined by Napoleon who built up first-class bases up-Channel at Cherbourg and Antwerp.

'Steam has bridged the Channel'

During the eighteenth century the Royal Navy had become the most powerful in the world and after 1815 it was in an unchallenged position. Then came decline. As British overseas posses-

sions grew during the reign of the Queen Empress, the navy was inadequate to satisfy all the demands made upon it. Part of the problem was a conservatism which only slowly made allowance for technical innovation matched by the parsimony of the Treasury. What was lacking in warship design and armaments in the first half of the century, however, did not apply to infrastructure at the dockyards and anchorages. The construction of artificial harbours of refuge which had begun in the previous century at Ramsgate was followed by the Plymouth Breakwater, begun in 1811 and completed in 1848 at great expense (**13**). After this came massive works to create Portland Harbour in mid century. The construction of a vast, fortified, potentially hostile harbour at Cherbourg influenced the beginning of the Alderney harbour of refuge in reaction. Earlier, the building of the Royal William Victualling Yard at Plymouth (1825–34) provided the means to replenish an Atlantic fleet; while in Portsmouth, the construction of the Block Mills inaugurated the mass-production process in an

already highly industrialized dockyard. Similar improvements were taking place in Chatham and Sheerness.

To these initiatives must be added the introduction of steam-power to wooden ships and eventually to ironclad warships as well as the influence of the rifled and shell-firing gun. That steam-power had made the warship no longer so susceptible to wind and tide appeared to some, erroneously, to give greater advantage to the attacker. It produced the dramatic observation from Lord Palmerston that 'steam has bridged the Channel'.

Between 1859 and 1868 great energy went into reconstructing the navy as well as attending to the previously outdated coastal defences. The incentive came with the launching of *La Gloire* by the French, to be countered by *Warrior*. The earlier application of iron to warships led to greater attention to armour-plate as a reaction to improved gunnery. The development of the centre-line gun turret followed, which allowed wider deployment and protection of the guns and

13 *Plymouth Breakwater and Fort. The armoured fort was built on a rock behind Rennie's breakwater in the 1860s.*

made the broadside armament obsolete. The effects of the Crimean War (1853–6) stimulated the controversy regarding the claims to the superiority of ships over coastal batteries. There were also lessons to be learnt from the American Civil War (1861–5), particularly in the use of ironclads. That war also stimulated new submarine weapons such as underwater mines which had so disturbed the Royal Navy when its ships were in the channels before Kronstadt during the northern campaign of the war with Russia.

There was a reaction to the 1860 Royal Commission's recommendations on coastal fortifications especially from the navalists who focused on the Spithead sea-forts, claiming that they were unnecessary and ineffective (**14**). Captain Cowper Phipps Coles advanced an alternative defence using floating batteries. Blue Water theories were later put forward more effectively in the professional journals of the time. The navy was held to

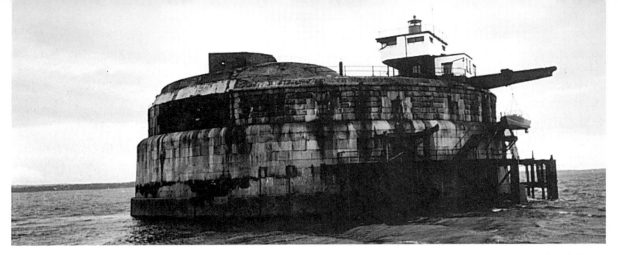

14 *Spitbank Fort, with iron-faced casemates towards the entrance to the Solent.*

be 'the shield to guard, and the army is the spear to strike'. Colonel Sir John Colomb and Sir Charles Dilke in parliament repeated the Nelsonian doctrine that the frontier of a naval power was the coastline of her foe. The navy, in the 1870s and 1880s, though suffering from the policy of financial retrenchment pursued by the Liberal government under Gladstone, was not seriously challenged at the time by foreign fleets.

In 1884 W. T. Stead, as editor of the *Pall Mall Gazette*, produced a powerful series of articles – 'The Truth about the Navy by One Who Knows the Facts'. Awareness that the navy was no longer absolutely confident of preventing an invasion in certain circumstances led to a new popular scare. A colossal interservice row ensued between the rival schools of thought. The army faction was convinced that France could mobilize and embark 100,000 men within a week. The Director of Military Intelligence in 1888 affirmed:

> if the French could obtain complete command of the Channel for three weeks, they could collect in their northern ports enough tonnage to transport 150,000 infantry and supplies across the Channel.

It would only take two trips to bring the infantry. In that year, extraordinary naval preparations were taken at Toulon to add to the tension. Yet the army and naval estimates of 1889 showed

that the 'Blue Water School' had won the debate. The resulting Naval Defence Act led to 8 new battleships being built, 38 cruisers of varying size and fast torpedo-carrying vessels or fleet escorts besides.

The Admiralty and War Office remained at loggerheads over the invasion issue until the Committee of Imperial Defence was created in 1903. It was a time when the nature of naval warfare was changing. The use of fast torpedo boats capable of rapid raids into harbours and anchorages demanded the deployment of quick-firing guns and searchlights (**15**). The establishment of French torpedo boat stations between Dunkirk

15 *Tilbury Fort: 12-pounder quick-firing guns restored to the late nineteenth-century rampart.*

16 *Brennan Torpedo (Royal Engineers Museum, Chatham).*

and Brest reinforced popular fears in Britain (see **8**). Counter-measures led to land based torpedoes of the Brennan type (**16**) which were sited to defend estuaries such as the Thames and Medway and individual harbours (**17**). Boom defences were also installed. In 1898 came the success of the French submarine *Gustave Zédé*. By 1902, the *Navy and Army Illustrated* was featuring Britain's new submarine squadron and so a new dimension was added to naval warfare.

The emphasis was now heavily on the side of the Royal Navy as the race with Germany for more and more dreadnoughts heightened by the end of the century. 'The Navy is the 1st, 2nd, 3rd, 4th, 5th . . . ad infinitum Line of Defence! If the Navy is not supreme, no Army however large is of the slightest use. It is not *invasion* we have to fear if our Navy is beaten, IT'S STARVATION!' said Admiral Fisher in 1904.

The Channel in two world wars

During the twentieth century the potential enemy changed from France to Germany so that in 1914 the Grand Fleet was based on Scapa Flow, Orkney, and controlled the approaches to the east coast. The Channel Fleet still operated south and west from Dover. Two weeks after the assassination at Sarajevo, ships of the Royal Navy began to assemble at Portland. On 28 July the fleet was ordered to its war station at Scapa Flow.

There had been a change in the harbour facilities at the eastern end of the English Channel too. The harbour of refuge at Dover, which had been long proposed, was begun in 1897 and completed in 1909. It was to be of great significance for naval tactics in the two world wars to come.

In 1914 there was a total of 26 defended ports. There was still the feeling, among soldiers at any rate, that naval protection alone was not adequate insurance against attack. Lord Morley's subcommittee of 1907–8 put the maximum strength of the likely invader at 70,000 men and this figure was used as a rule of thumb for some considerable time. Above that figure it was assumed that the navy could deal with the invading force. At a more local level, the Dover Patrol and light forces stationed at Harwich guarded the passage to

17 *Cliffe Fort Brennan Torpedo station: launching rail outside the fort.*

Flanders. The Nore Defence Flotilla consisted of elderly destroyers and torpedo boats. Home waters were divided into twenty-three patrol areas.

During the first war Dover was a base for submarines and for a patrol with responsibility for preventing German submarines passing through the Straits. A new wartime port for supplying Flanders was created at Richborough. The Dover Patrol provided protection for the barge and train ferry traffic from there to the Continent and for routine convoy duties.

As the German submarine menace became more devastating, two lines of defence across the Channel were created, from Abbots Cliff to Cap Grisnez with a continuous line of drifters equipped with magnesium flares, which, with powerful searchlights such as those on the cliffs at Folkestone and on vessels in the Channel, provided a serious threat to the night movement of submarines. There was a mine barrage off Dover specifically against U-boats.

It was also important to protect Portland Harbour against submarine attack. In November 1914 the old turret battleship *Hood* was sunk across the southern entrance of the harbour after the loss of *Formidable*. Such was the growing damage to merchant shipping that an anti-submarine division of the Admiralty was formed. Specially disguised merchant 'Q' ships were armed. Royal Naval Air Service stations flew anti-submarine patrols. Portland was part of the Portsmouth group which established its headquarters at Calshot in 1917 and included another substation at Bembridge, Isle of Wight. Additional stations were created at Newhaven and Lee-on-the-Solent for seaplanes; Polegate for airships; and balloons at Tipnor. There was a naval airship station at Capel near Dover.

After the First War, naval strategy in the years leading up to 1939 was based on ensuring the successful defence of the British Isles and the sea-routes which supplied so much of Britain's food and raw materials. The reshaping of the maritime defences, however, made little progress before the mid 1930s. The creation of Coastal Command identified its flying duties as trade protection, reconnaissance and co-operation with the Royal Navy.

Maritime defence in home waters consisted of four commands: Western Approaches (Plymouth), Portsmouth Command; the Nore Command (Chatham) and the coast of Scotland (Rosyth). Portland assumed a much greater importance with elements of the Channel Force stationed there in 1939. The headquarters of Coastal Command was at Lee-on-the-Solent. (see **9**)

In 1940 the fall of France meant that to some degree the Royal Navy had lost control of the Narrow Seas. The Dover mine barrage, which had been so significant in the first war, became largely ineffective because German ships could now avoid it by hugging the French coast. In June the Home Fleet was much depleted and consisted of 5 battleships, 11 cruisers and 80 destroyers. Local forces in the neighbourhood of the anticipated landing places were said to be very weak. The Nore Command had only 19 destroyers at the Humber, Harwich and Sheerness and twice that number were thought to be necessary by the Chiefs of Staff. Dover and Portsmouth had 5 destroyers each. Apart from the heavy ships, cruiser and flotilla forces, 25 fast minesweepers and 140 minesweeping trawlers were responsible for maintaining the searched channels between Sunderland and Portsmouth. There was also an Auxiliary Patrol of up to 400 trawlers and small craft disposed about the coast between Invergordon and Portland to give warning of approaching hostile forces and attack

them. In addition, there were about 100 Harbour Defence Patrol craft. Altogether about 700 armed patrol vessels of one sort or another were available for offshore reconnaissance. Much of the naval provision was allocated to the east coast, the heavier ships based on Scapa Flow or Rosyth. The destroyers were organized in four flotillas based on the Humber, Harwich, Sheerness and Dover or Portsmouth. By the end of July the Nore Command had an increase of 32 destroyers.

As the summer wore on and the pressure created by Operation 'Sealion' intensified, the danger from the direction of Norway and the German ports lessened and the build-up of invasion barges became concentrated on the area between Ostend and Boulogne. This gave greater focus for aggressive/defensive activity with attacks by sea and air on the invasion barges repeating tactics of previous centuries.

After the immediate threat of invasion had lifted there were still hostile measures at sea which had to be countered. Minelaying and submarine warfare were always present, but so were fast torpedo-carrying E-boats, and the coastal batteries as far west as Portland and Falmouth could be called on to engage them up to the time of the D-Day landings (**colour plate 6**).

The preparations for the Allied landings in France have themselves left their physical traces particularly for the construction and deployment of landing craft as well as the prefabricated sections of the Mulberry Harbour at places such as Hayling Island and Portland Harbour. While these represent the offensive rather than the defensive aspects of the second war, they form part of the naval side of the archaeological record in the English Channel.

3
Defence of the naval bases

The emergence of a permanent Royal Navy under the first Tudor kings changed the pattern of coastal defence. During the Middle Ages, individual ports and sea-coast towns might have their own fortifications of walls, towers and chain booms across harbour mouths but there was no overall national defence strategy. From the sixteenth century to the First World War, the fortified naval bases and anchorages were at the core of Britain's permanent fixed defences. This concept lay behind the 'Devyce', the programme of fortification prepared by Henry VIII's advisers, and was at the root of the report of the Royal Commission on the Defences of the United Kingdom published in 1860; the most comprehensive statement of defence policy that, up to then, had ever been undertaken. That report provided a detailed catalogue of recommendations for the individual naval ports in the light of contemporary technological changes in sea-power and weaponry. The naval bases remained at the heart of defence strategy thereafter. Systematic protection of the commercial ports was considered later in the nineteenth century. Otherwise, it has only been at moments of imminent danger that wider measures to combat invasion have been put in place and they are described in the next chapter.

The likelihood of full-scale invasion was remote during the Middle Ages; coastal raids were more common. Surviving harbour medieval defences can be seen along the Channel coast from the mud walls of Sandwich, Kent, the

18 *The Round Tower, Portsmouth Point. The early fifteenth-century tower was later heightened and refaced. Across the entrance to Portsmouth Harbour are the casemates of Fort Blockhouse.*

Round Tower at Portsmouth Point (**18**), to the towers which guarded the ends of the chain across Fowey Harbour, Cornwall. The best example of this form of defence is Dartmouth Castle, Devon, where there is a long and continuous story (**19**). A castle or fortified house on the western side of the harbour entrance was being built in 1388 by John Hawley, a mayor of Dartmouth and thought to be the model for Chaucer's shipman in *The Canterbury Tales*. Lengths of curtain-wall and an angle tower still remain behind St Petrox Church but this 'fortalice' was inadequate as a harbour defence and was replaced by the present tower begun in 1481. This is perhaps the first fortification in England which was built for the use of heavy guns. These were mounted at basement level to command the sea. During the previous century or so the introduction of gunpowder weapons to defences had only led to the provision of small loops for hand-

19 *Dartmouth Castle from Kingswear. The round and square towers of the 1480s' castle are on the water's edge. Behind is the high curtain-wall of the fourteenth-century castle and to the left is the mid-nineteenth-century battery.*

guns in walls and towers. As well as this innovation, the castle carries the impression of the windlass mechanism which controlled the chain boom supported by small boats across the harbour at times of emergency. Dartmouth Castle was matched a few years later by Kingswear Castle on the opposite shore. Subsequently, the tower of Dartmouth Castle was supplemented by external gun batteries alongside as weaponry improved during the sixteenth century. Eighteenth-century open batteries on the headland were replaced in 1861 by a substantial casemated battery for five rifled muzzle loaders (RMLs) and the local Artillery Volunteers continued to use the battery for practice during the

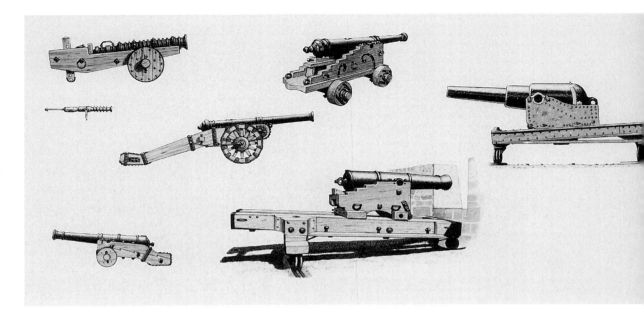

remainder of the century. Finally, the upper level of the battery was adapted to take two 4.7-inch quick-firing guns during the Second World War.

Such was Dartmouth's medieval legacy, which could continue to be serviceable by virtue of its topographical situation, but this was local rather than national defence. For as long as the navy was regarded as the first line of the country's defence the need for secure bases was fundamental. The many activities performed by the navy required shipbuilding slips and dry docks where warships could be repaired, maintained and supplied. Alongside the yards there developed the organizations for armament supply and victualling. All this meant that the naval bases held great quantities of naval stores and supplies of all kinds. They were vulnerable to attack from long-range bombardment by warships, or from close-quarters assault from a military force put ashore in the vicinity.

The defence of dockyards, therefore, was a long-term commitment, which reflected the evolving process of military engineering. As the establishment of dockyards and naval bases developed in the seventeenth century, and particularly during the eighteenth, the main elements of English coastal defence took shape. The significance of individual yards changed as the direction from which danger threatened shifted. Improvements in the efficiency of weapons and in the methods of attack inevitably led to new concepts of defence. The building of individual castles and blockhouses during the sixteenth century eventually proved insufficient. By the seventeenth century, dockyards were beginning to be enclosed by lines of bastioned fortifications as well as being protected by adjacent coastal batteries. This process of enclosure and all-round defence was developed in the eighteenth century on a more elaborate scale and had to take into account the expansion of the dockyard facilities themselves. Commanding positions outside the dockyard had also to be defended. As the range and effectiveness of artillery increased in the mid-nineteenth century so the defensive ring was taken further and further outwards to keep a hostile force beyond bombardment range. This expansion of dockyard defences is first recognizable during the eighteenth century, mainly to cover potential landing places nearby, and then more dramatically in the second half of the nineteenth century, as the rifled gun and the explosive shell revolutionized warfare (**20**). By the end of the nineteenth century close defence of dockyards returned because of the danger posed by fast torpedo boats in addition to enemy long-range guns.

20 *Coast artillery across 350 years. Examples of the main types of guns used in coastal batteries:*
(i) wrought-iron breech-loading gun of the 1540s;
(ii) sixteenth-century wrought-iron swivel gun;
(iii) cast-iron saker of the late 1540s on a ship carriage;
(iv) mid-sixteenth-century cast-iron gun on a field carriage;
(v) late seventeenth-century gun on a fortress carriage;
(vi) nineteenth-century traversing carriage with 64-pounder gun;

(vii) rifled wrought-iron gun developed in the 1850s by Sir William Armstrong;
(viii) late nineteenth-century gun on a hydro-pneumatic disappearing carriage;
(ix) 6-inch gun of the 1890s;
(x) quick firing 6- and 12-pounder guns used against fast torpedo boats

(drawings by Sarson and Bryan).

This meant a return to the use of booms and to submarine mining and land-based torpedoes, together with defence electric lights and quick firing guns.

Portsmouth, at a central point along the Channel, was the site of the longest-established naval base following the order from Henry VII for the construction of a dry dock there in 1495. At Deptford and Woolwich there were shipbuilding yards, and five blockhouses sited at Tilbury and Gravesend to cross their fire over the Thames protected them as well as the approaches to London. The next naval base was the Elizabethan creation at Chatham followed by two smaller yards at Harwich and the late seventeenth-century Sheerness. Dock (later Devonport) near Plymouth was the last of the south-coast dockyards and was begun in the 1690s. During the

eighteenth century, Portsmouth and Plymouth had risen to equal importance leaving Chatham a poor third. Sheerness was subordinate to Chatham because of its cramped site. Sheerness had, however, caused the closure of the Harwich dockyard by 1713. The War of the Austrian Succession (1740–8) emphasized the importance of the south-coast yards but it was the Seven Years War (1756–63) which also highlighted their inadequacies leading to much needed expansion and reorganization towards the end of the century. In the mid-nineteenth century came the massive expansion of the yards to cope with the development of the Victorian steam navy.

The warships were themselves vulnerable when 'in ordinary' or out of commission at their moorings or while being refitted and repaired – a frequent necessity for timber vessels. Strategic anchorages had also to be denied to an enemy, and this was especially so for the more remote, such as the Isles of Scilly whose situation in hostile hands could disrupt communications with Ireland, threaten the approaches to the Channel or could even be used as a privateering base. At the eastern end of the Channel was the strip of reasonably sheltered water between the Goodwin Sands and the land known as the Downs, opposite Deal and Walmer. Such anchorages were also vital to merchant shipping especially when being assembled for convoy.

The importance of defending anchorages was recognized as a priority in 1539. The most extensive of Henry's fortifications were 'the three castles which keep the Downs' – Deal, Walmer and Sandown (**colour plate 6**). Other important anchorages protected in Henry's scheme were Weymouth Bay and the Fal Estuary. Anchorages much used in the eighteenth century were St Helens, off the north-eastern tip of the Isle of Wight, Torbay and Cawsand on the west side of Plymouth Sound.

In more recent times, artificial harbours – harbours of refuge – were created. Ramsgate, at the end of the eighteenth century, provided security during bad weather between the anchorages of the Nore (at the point where the Thames and Medway Estuaries meet) and that of the Downs. In the nineteenth century the construction of the breakwater at Portland (completed in 1872) provided shelter and facilities for the navy which led to the establishment of a base specializing in torpedo development and ultimately as an anti-submarine establishment in the two world wars (**21**). Plymouth Breakwater, which protected the Sound, had been completed in 1848 (see **13**). Alderney was begun in 1845 in response to the French initiatives at Cherbourg. Finally at the end of the century came the great harbour works at Dover.

Defended anchorages

Before looking at the developing defences of the naval dockyards it is logical to examine the protection of the main anchorages along the

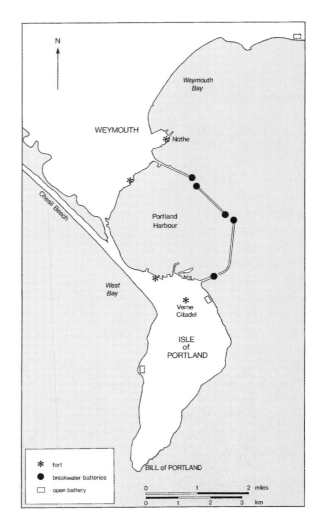

21 *Map of Portland Harbour defences.*

Channel coast since these were the first locations to receive attention. From east to west they included the Thames and Medway Estuaries, the Downs, Portland or Weymouth Bay, Torbay, Falmouth and the Isles of Scilly. The anchorages closely associated with the naval dockyards of Portsmouth and Plymouth will be considered later.

When coastal defence on a national scale was first put into effect it was during the political crisis of 1538–9. Invasion threatened and the king's ships patrolled the coasts; the early-warning beacon system was mobilized and commissioners were sent out to identify potential landing places.

New fortifications, permanent as well as emergency trenches and batteries, were built along the south coast from the Thames to the Fal Estuary to deny the enemy a supply base to sustain an invasion.

Henry VIII's 'castles'

Henry VIII's coastal castles of 1539–40 are familiar landmarks. Of 'the three castles which keep the Downs' Deal and Walmer Castles remain in their essential detail, despite their later conversion into official seaside residences. Sandown has almost entirely been eroded by the sea. Sandgate Castle, near Folkestone, has also suffered from erosion and its central tower was converted into a Martello tower at the time of a later invasion crisis. Camber Castle, west of Rye (Sussex), is now a substantial ruin beside a long-silted harbour. Southsea Castle commands the deep-water channel approaching Portsmouth Harbour, and two blockhouses of East and West Cowes commanded, the entrance to the Medina on the Isle of Wight. Only the western of these blockhouses survives as the clubhouse of the Royal Yacht Squadron. A castle at Sandown defended the potential landing place in the bay. Calshot Castle guarded the entrance to Southampton Water (**22**) and Hurst Castle commanded the Needles passage. Moving westward to Weymouth Bay, Portland Castle is well preserved but its slightly later partner on the north side of the bay, Sandsfoot Castle, has partly collapsed through cliff erosion. Pendennis and St Mawes Castles on either side of Falmouth Harbour remain complete in all essentials.

22 *Calshot Castle from the north-west, at the entrance to Southampton Water.*

23 *Deal Castle as envisaged* c. *1545, by Alan Sorrell.*

These 'castles' were all compact, solidly built, masonry towers, often with attached, rounded bastions up to six in number (Deal) (**23**). They retained certain characteristic medieval features such as drawbridges and portcullis but they also have profound differences. They were conceived primarily as a means for mounting tiers of heavy guns; they were therefore an acknowledgement of the decisive new weapon of gunpowder artillery that had slowly become the dominant weapon in warfare during the course of the fifteenth century. Their many common features suggest a single hand in their design even if there are variations in the basic plan. Although the designer of the somewhat idiosyncratic Camber Castle is known – a Bohemian engineer, Stephan von Haschenperg – we do not know the authorship of the others, though the king himself was closely involved. They are all concentric, their plan dominated by a circular or multangular tower, with an outer and lower gun battery which in most cases consists of a variable number of rounded bastions. In each 'castle' there are never less than three tiers of guns. At Deal there are five tiers. The fire-power may also be divided between those guns directed at a distant target and those providing close defence, covering outer dry moats and internal courtyards. Almost every external feature is rounded whether towers, bastions or the parapets as though the emphasis is to deflect incoming shot. Some original partitions and internal features survive in places.

The theoretical basis for the design may be influenced by a treatise on military engineering printed at Amsterdam in 1527 by the German Renaissance polymath Albrecht Dürer. In many respects these massive masonry 'castles' appear to be outmoded by comparison with the 'modern' angle-bastion fortification emanating from Italy during the early sixteenth century and which reflected the changed nature of land warfare. The function of Henry's castles, however, was to combat ships. In their isolated situations commanding harbours, with their ability to provide all-round defence and their prodigious fire-power if fully armed, they were formidable fortresses which, in various ways, were retained as forts in later centuries despite their blatant anachronism.

The great 'castles' were just one form of fortification associated with Henry's coastal defence programme. There were the more numerous and smaller blockhouses, usually D-shaped towards the front with rectangular garrison accommodation to the rear. These had some of the characteristics of the 'castles' but did not have the same capacity for all-round self-defence. Sandsfoot Castle (Weymouth) was a larger version of such a blockhouse; West Cowes Castle and Brownsea Island Castle are others. The smaller blockhouses tend not to survive. Two examples, however, are sited by the water's edge below Pendennis and St Mawes Castles. At Little Dennis the blockhouse is complete apart from its roof and floor.

The excavated half of the Gravesend blockhouse can still be seen on the Thames waterfront. It is all that is now visible of the five blockhouses which defended the approaches to London.

There were also circular earth 'bulwarks' in the intervals between the Downs 'castles', linked by a trench (**24**). These were sketched in the early eighteenth century but there is now no trace. Archaeological excavation suggests that the

24 *Bird's eye view of the earthwork bulwarks and connecting trench between Deal and Walmer Castles as sketched by William Stukeley in 1725.*

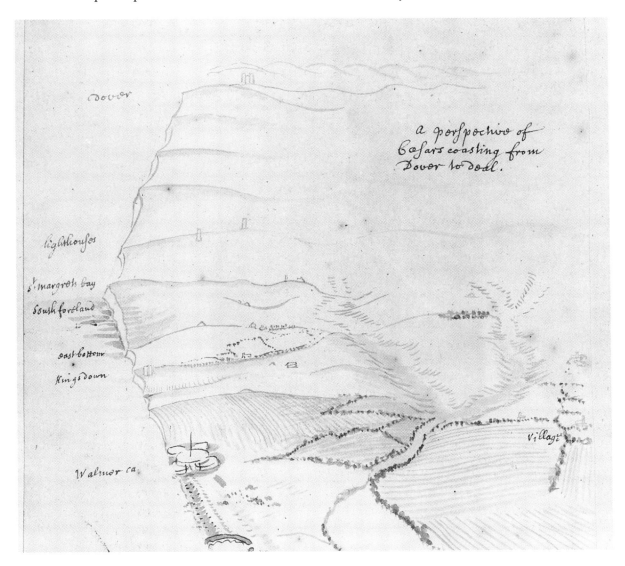

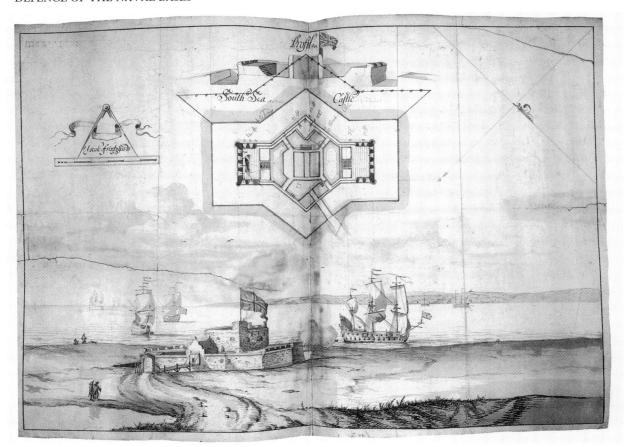

25 *Plan and view of Southsea Castle in the 1670s by Thomas Phillips.*

Thames blockhouses also had associated earthworks and earthen batteries but such features tend not to survive at ground level.

The circular plan and thick, somewhat high masonry walls, which were such a feature of Henry's 'castles', were part of a mainly northern European tradition that, by the 1540s, was already outdated. The low-lying, earth-backed curtain-walls, broad enough to manoeuvre cannon and flanked at intervals by projecting, sharply angled bastions, which had been developed by Italian engineers at the beginning of the sixteenth century, were already proving to be the best defensive devices against the weapons of the day. By the end of Henry's reign (1547), the new Italian bastion system, or at least some of its angled forms, had infiltrated English military thinking and transitional examples can still be seen in the plan of Southsea Castle (**25**) and at Yarmouth Castle in the Isle of Wight.

An up-to-the-minute example of the Italian fortress plan with its recessed flanking guns masked by the projecting ears (orillons) of the bastion was drawn up in 1551 for the protection of the anchorage of St Mary's Pool, Isles of Scilly. In practice, this drawing-office product was too large for the hilltop the fort was meant to occupy, so that all that remains today of the unfinished fort called Harry's Walls are two bastions and the intervening curtain (**26**). Elsewhere in Scilly, on the island of Tresco above the harbour of New Grimsby, was an old-fashioned blockhouse somewhat similar to Brownsea or Sandsfoot Castles and confusingly called King Charles's Castle, built at the same time. Its function was taken over by the mid-seventeenth-century tower, Cromwell's Castle, built at sea-level (**27**)

26 *Harry's Walls, St Mary's, Isles of Scilly. Plan of 1551 but only one length of curtain and two orillon bastions were built because the fort as planned was badly sited.*

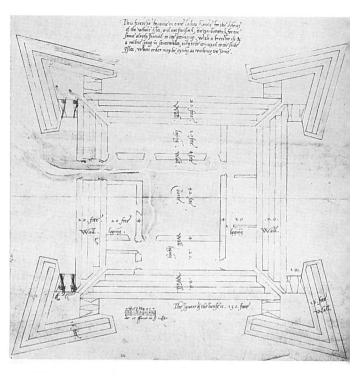

Medway and Thames

As the Elizabethan navy became established as a permanent service, an anchorage was found for it in the Medway when 'in ordinary'. This was below Rochester Bridge in Chatham Reach. Some store buildings were erected at Chatham and were the precursor of the later dockyard. One of Elizabeth's early acts as queen was to commission the building of a fort at Upnor on the north bank, opposite Chatham, 'for the safeguard of our navy'. Initially Upnor Castle consisted of a great angled bastion projecting into the river at full tide with a rectangular residential block on the low cliff behind having a waterfront façade of tall, slender towers (see **4**). It was designed by the leading English engineer of the day, Sir Richard Lee, who was responsible for the

27 *Cromwell's Castle, Tresco, Isles of Scilly. Gun tower of the 1650s built to control the anchorage of New Grimsby between Tresco and Bryher.*

up-to-date Italian-style defences of Berwick-upon-Tweed. At Upnor, however, the use of a bastion as the basis for a riverside battery was not the most effective use of the form and the turreted façade seems anachronistic. Its land front was improved at the end of Elizabeth's reign.

After the Dutch raid on the Medway in 1667, Upnor Castle was replaced by more powerful batteries further downstream at Cockham Wood and Gillingham Forts (see **5**). The two-tiered battery of Cockham Wood can still be seen, though it is largely overgrown and its lower battery is eroded by the river (**28**). Two centuries later, these batteries were superseded by two 1860s' granite-faced, casemated forts (Darnet and Hoo) on low islands even further downstream.

28 *Reconstruction drawing of Cockham Wood Fort, one of the batteries designed by Sir Bernard de Gomme to defend the Medway.*

A similar process of front lines moving in stages downstream can be seen in the Thames Estuary. The West Tilbury Blockhouse was replaced on the same site by the impressive Tilbury Fort built in the 1670s and 1680s by Charles II's Chief Engineer, Sir Bernard de Gomme (**colour plate 7**). This is a fine pentagonal bastioned fort in classic Old Dutch style with complex outworks consisting of a covered way and double wet moats. Its water-gate has a great baroque frontispiece and inside are eighteenth-century barracks and powder magazines. Its riverside gun-lines were matched by a simpler battery now known as New Tavern Fort at Gravesend.

At the end of the eighteenth century earthwork advance batteries were built downstream. These were subsumed by an advanced line of the 1860s (**29**). Coalhouse Fort at East Tilbury on the Essex bank is the most accessible of three, single-tier casemated batteries. Tilbury and New Tavern

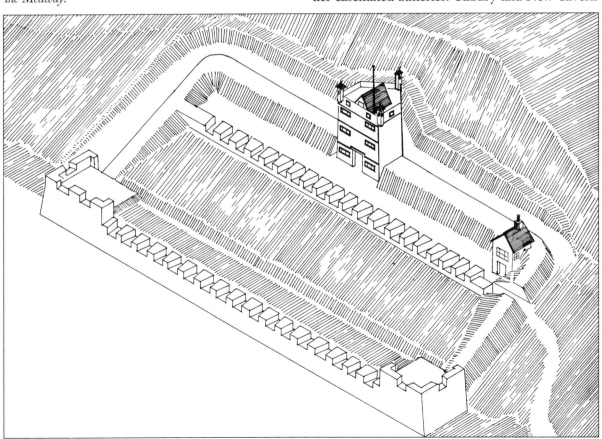

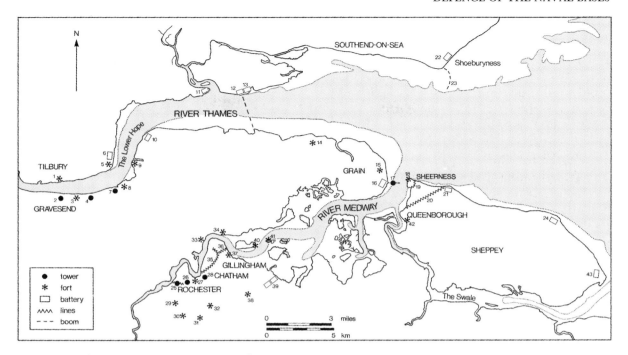

29 *Map of Thames and Medway defences: 1 Tilbury Fort;*
2 Gravesend Blockhouse; 3 New Tavern Fort; 4 Milton
Blockhouse; 5 Coalhouse Fort; 6 East Tilbury Battery;
7 Higham Blockhouse; 8 Shornemead Fort; 9 Cliffe Fort;
10 Lower Hope Point Batteries; 11 Shellhaven Battery;
12 Scar's Elbow Battery; 13 Deadman's Battery;
14 Slough Fort; 15 Grain Fort; 16 Grain Battery;
17 Grain Tower; 18 Garrison Point Fort; 19 Sheerness
Lines; 20 Queenborough Lines; 21 Barton's Point Battery;

22 Shoeburyness Battery; 23 Shoeburyness Boom;
24 Fletcher and Warden Point Batteries; 25 Fort Clarence;
26 Delce Tower; 27 Fort Pitt; 28 Gibraltar Tower;
29 Fort Borstal; 30 Fort Bridgewoods; 31 Fort Horstead;
32 Fort Luton; 33 Upnor Castle; 34 Cockham Wood Fort;
35 Fort Amherst; 36 Chatham Lines; 37 Gillingham Fort;
38 Fort Darland; 39 Twydall Redoubts; 40 Hoo Fort;
41 Darnet Fort; 42 Queenborough Castle;
43 Shellness Battery.

Forts were relegated to the second line but both were rearmed with rifled muzzle loaders, and Tilbury was later equipped with 12-pounder quick-firers (see **15**).

Portland and Falmouth

Towards the western end of the Channel, the much used anchorage of Torbay (Devon) was protected during the 1780s by three detached batteries armed with a total of twenty 20-pounder guns on Berry Head above Brixham. But the earlier anchorages of Portland and Falmouth, which had been fortified by Henry VIII, were completely reordered in the latter half of the nineteenth century when greater gun ranges meant an extended shift of the defences to the harbour mouths.

Portland Roads only provided shelter from south-westerlies and its value as an anchorage was limited. As early as 1795, John Harvey of Weymouth had suggested the idea of a breakwater. The decision to put this into practice eventually came in 1844 and work began in 1847. A new prison at Portland was built for the purpose of providing the labour for the project. The southern arm was the first part to be built and the last stone of the breakwater was laid on 3 March 1871.

The defences of the new harbour were designed in 1857, stimulated by the threat from France whose naval base at Cherbourg had just been strongly fortified along with an investment in ironclad warships. At Portland itself the

30 *Nothe Fort, Weymouth, under construction in the 1860s.*

defences comprised the Verne Citadel (now a prison) rising above the East Weare batteries firing across the bay. The circular Breakwater Fort was intended for 14 guns, the Inner Pier Head Fort for 8 guns, and the Nothe Fort on the Weymouth side complemented the East Weare guns. The later Breakwater batteries (A, B and C Pierheads) were added when the construction of the centre and north arms of the breakwater were sanctioned in 1893 (see **21**).

Although its present use as a prison prevents a public view of the interior of the Verne Citadel, its massive earthworks can be appreciated externally. The enormous ditch is 120 ft (36.6m) wide and 70 ft (21m) deep at its greatest extent. It served partially as a stone quarry for the construction of the breakwater. The fort's irregular shape was dictated by the lie of the land. It was well defended towards the land and its ditches could be raked by fire from bombproof caponiers within the ditch. It was built to house all the troops needed for the defence of the harbour. The Nothe Fort, on the Weymouth side, is not so extensive and is a more conventional sea battery. It is a large casemated work and in 1872 four 9-inch and six 10-inch rifled muzzle loaders were installed here (**30**). It has now been restored and is vividly displayed through local efforts.

At first there was no intention of providing a naval base at Portland. However, the shelter and facilities of the harbour enabled the navy to carry out experimental work at Portland and early on there was a training establishment. Whitehead's Torpedo factory was built at Wyke Regis and opened in 1891 and the navy established a torpedo depot in the dockyard in 1901.

The British fleet was itself vulnerable to torpedo attack and new defences were proposed for both Portland and the new harbour at Dover. Additional breakwaters were needed at Portland to enclose the harbour fully. These were completed by 1906 but initially there was simply a line of dolphins of timber and iron with nets stretched between them as a temporary defence. It was thought that Portland was susceptible to a night attack from torpedo boats and the harbour was equipped with electric fighting lights and 12-pounder quick-firers on the Pierhead batteries. New batteries for long-range, breech-loading guns were built at Blacknor and Upton in the early 1900s to cover the western and eastern approaches respectively. In May 1912 Portland was the location for a grand assembly and review of the Fleet, and by the outbreak of war in 1914 an enclosed and defended naval base had largely been achieved (see **21**).

At Falmouth there is a similar sequence of shifts in emphasis. There was a move during the Napoleonic Wars to advance the batteries beyond the confines of the Henrician castles. This was later emphasized in 1897 with batteries for 6-inch breech-loaders at Half Moon Battery below Pendennis Castle (**colour plate 8**) and at St Anthony Head to keep enemy cruisers at a distance. A battery for four 12-pounder quick-firers behind St Mawes Castle was completed in

1903 to defend the entrance from torpedo-boat attack. This latter battery replaced an earlier 6-pounder battery on the cliff below the castle for the defence of a submarine minefield. Continuity was maintained during the Second World War when new quick-firer batteries and searchlight positions were built at St Mawes and Middle Point, Pendennis (**31**).

The Isles of Scilly have a long history of fortification. Following upon the defences of Edward VI's reign fortifications had developed on the Hugh, St Mary's, at the end of the sixteenth century, commanding both the harbour and the principal approach by St Mary's Sound. Extensive earthwork defences were thrown up by the royalist garrison at the end of the Civil War and afterwards Cromwell's Castle was built on Tresco (see **27**). The bastioned lines on the Hugh, St Mary's, were substantially replaced in stone during the first half of the eighteenth century. Later, as a measure to combat the threat of French torpedo boats at the end of the nineteenth century, short-lived 6-inch breech-loader and quick-firer

31 *Pendennis Headland, Falmouth. The eighteenth-century and later Crab Quay Battery with World War II searchlight bases below; to the far left is Little Dennis Blockhouse.*

batteries were built; while in two world wars seaplane bases and an airfield for fighters were constructed as an anti-U-boat outpost.

Portsmouth

Of the three great southern naval bases the defences of Portsmouth are the most extensive, including as they do the Isle of Wight (**32**). They

are also among the best preserved and most publicly accessible. The majority of the fortifications belong to the nineteenth century but all the main periods of construction are represented so it is possible to follow the course of defensive measures across the centuries.

From 1416 to 1422, the entrance to Portsmouth Harbour was protected by a chain boom guarded

32 *Map of Portsmouth and Isle of Wight defences:*
1 *Needles and New Needles Batteries;* 2 *Hatherwood Battery;* 3 *Hurst Castle;* 4 *Warden Point Battery;*
5 *Fort Albert and Cliff End Battery;* 6 *Yarmouth Castle;*
7 *Fort Victoria;* 8 *Golden Hill Fort;* 9 *Freshwater Bay Redoubt;* 10 *Bouldner Battery;* 11 *Netley Castle;*
12 *St Andrew's Point;* 13 *Calshot Castle;* 14 *West Cowes Castle;* 15 *East Cowes Castle;* 16 *Carisbrooke Castle;*
17 *Fort Fareham;* 18 *Fort Gomer;* 19 *Fort Grange;*
20 *Fort Rowner;* 21 *Fort Brockhurst;* 22 *Fort Elson;*
23 *Fort Wallington;* 24 *Fort Nelson;* 25 *Portchester Castle;*

26 *Fort Southwick;* 27 *Fort Widley;* 28 *Fort Purbrook;*
29 *Farlington Redoubt;* 30 *Brown Down Battery;*
31 *Gilkicker Fort;* 32 *Fort Monckton;* 33 *Gosport Lines;*
34 *Fort Blockhouse;* 35 *Portsea Lines;* 36 *Round Tower and Point Battery;* 37 *Portsmouth Lines;* 38 *Hilsea Lines;*
39 *Southsea Castle;* 40 *Spitbank Fort;* 41 *No Man's Land Fort;* 42 *St Helen's Fort;* 43 *Horse Sand Fort;* 44 *Lumps Fort;* 45 *Eastney Batteries;* 46 *Fort Cumberland;*
47 *Puckpool Mortar Battery;* 48 *Barrack Battery;*
49 *Sandown Fort;* 50 *Yaverland Battery;* 51 *Redcliffe Battery;* 52 *Bembridge Fort;* 53 *Nodes Battery.*

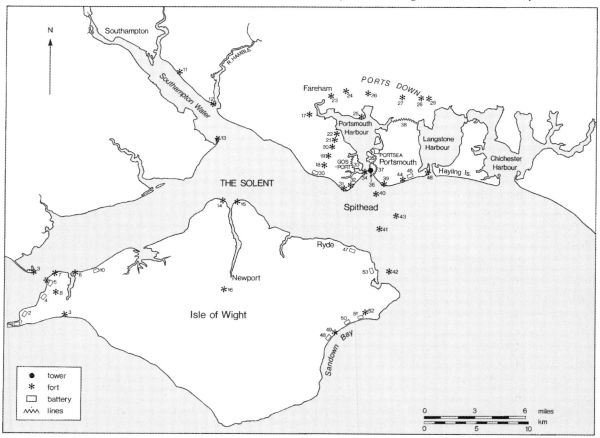

by a timber tower on the Gosport side and a masonry tower on Portsmouth Point. The Round Tower is still there, encased and heightened in later stonework, but still a distinct feature at the harbour entrance (see **18**). The enormous expanse of Portsmouth Harbour offered splendid opportunites for mooring medieval shipping and assembling fleets. At its head are the walls and bastions of the late Roman fort of Portchester associated with the defence of the 'Saxon Shore'. The fort stands virtually to full height and within one corner is the medieval royal castle which served as much to accommodate kings and their households on their travels to and from the Continent as a military establishment.

Henry VII's dockyard at Portsmouth initiated the concept of the defensible naval base which was at the core of British maritime policy, but for many years the dockyard itself lay outside the town whose defences protected instead the breweries, bakeries and storehouses vital for victualling the navy. The enclosing ditch and earth ramparts were begun in 1526, if not earlier, with the stone-built Square Tower of *c.* 1500 on the sea frontage, incorporated into the circuit. The town defences were improved in 1545 when the landward entrance received a rudimentary 'Italian' angle bastion – 'a great bastillion'. Under Elizabeth the town's 'mud walls' were remodelled to conform to the now well-established conventions of the bastion system, but defence was still focused on the enclosed town and the harbour entrance (**33**). Apart from Berwick-upon-Tweed, Portsmouth was the only English town to be fortified in a systematic and scientific manner in the Tudor period. When the town's defences were further improved by Charles II they were given a wider ditch and outworks together with a reworking of the bastions. As part of the reorganization and strengthening of the town defences in 1665, the Ordnance Office's Chief Engineer, Sir Bernard de Gomme, produced schemes for enclosing the dockyard within the wider fortifications. A simple version was in fact carried out but still left the dockyard distinct from the town and also gave no scope for the expansion of the

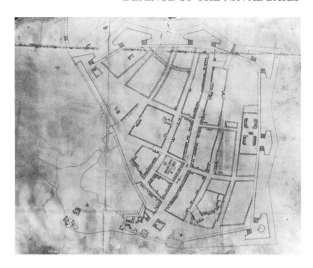

33 *Elizabethan defences of Portsmouth. Bastioned enceinte in the Italian style with orillon bastions replaced the Henrician defences. The Round Tower and the early seawards defences remain.*

dockyard's facilities. The town's fortified enceinte was again revised in the eighteenth century but the defences were almost entirely levelled in the years of Victorian urban expansion. The only visible stretch of the seventeenth-century works, apart from the Landport Gate and the resited King James's Gate, is King's Bastion and the Long Curtain on the sea-front.

The illustration of the French attempt on the Isle of Wight of 1545 shows a number of towers and bulwarks on the shore either side of the town. Chief of these is Southsea Castle sited to command the deep-water channel (see **3** and **25**). This is interesting as a transitional form of Henrician castle, concentric, but with a square central tower with two rectangular batteries, east and west, and large triangular salients towards the land and sea, instead of the familiar rounded bastions. Despite later alterations, its Tudor form is still distinct. It appropriately houses a museum relating to the town's defences.

Charles II's drive to improve the defences of Portsmouth extended to the Gosport side with a new battery on Blockhouse Point and the building of two small forts at the entrance to the harbour. Charles Fort was near the landing place

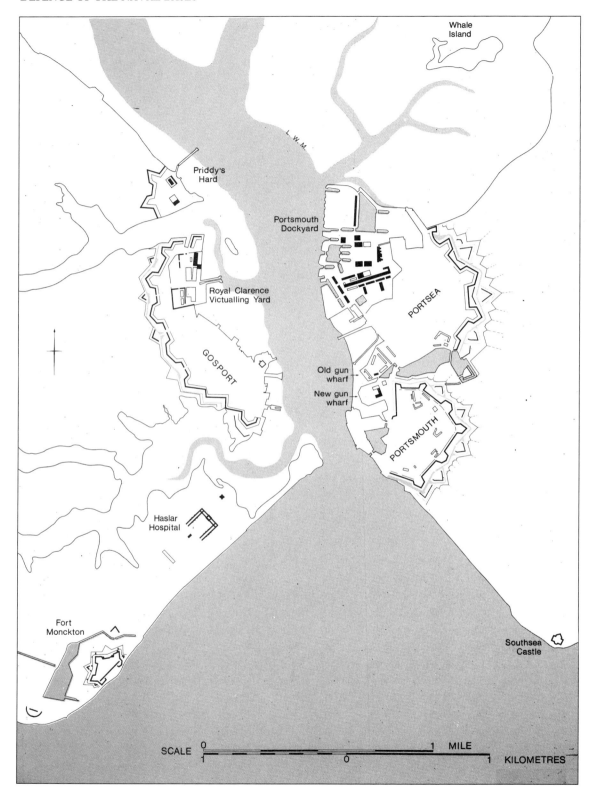

Whale
Island

L. W. M.

Priddy's
Hard

Portsmouth
Dockyard

PORTSEA

Royal Clarence
Victualling Yard

GOSPORT

Old gun
wharf

New gun
wharf

PORTSMOUTH

Haslar
Hospital

Fort
Monckton

Southsea
Castle

SCALE   0   1   MILE
         1   0   1   KILOMETRES

34 *Map of Portsmouth, Portsea and Gosport Lines protecting the dockyard and other naval establishments.*

at Gosport, the smaller James Fort was further into the harbour but neither survive. The town of Gosport was meant to have an elaborate bastioned front across the peninsula but this was only partially achieved at this date. To the north of Portsea Island, access was controlled by the checkpoint of Portsbridge Redoubt.

As the dockyard developed in the eighteenth century and expanded, so the houses of the dockyard workers began to appear on the neighbouring land known as Portsmouth Common. This settlement acquired its own name of Portsea and came to be included in a new bastioned defensive line. Although land was acquired by the Crown for the erection of new fortifications to protect the dockyard, nothing substantial was achieved until 1774–7. The new bastioned line included Portsea and linked up with the earlier defences of Portsmouth (**34**).

The defences of the naval base now began the sequence of expansion which was ultimately to lead to a fortified ring of 5 miles (8km) radius. It is these later works which survive most extensively. Under the intermittent pressures of war during the eighteenth century, the fortifications of Gosport were revised and enlarged. Parts of them still remain. The mood for dramatic improvement during the 1780s sprang from the strategic vision of the Duke of Richmond, Master General of the Ordnance. Though thwarted in parliament in his grand designs for Portsmouth and Plymouth, elements of his ideas did materialize. A small irregular earthwork named Fort Cumberland was constructed on the tip of Eastney Point where the eastern end of Portsea Island was believed to be open to attack and the entrance to Langstone Harbour unprotected. This little fort was replaced by a much larger Fort Cumberland in the 1790s, whose brick revetted ramparts, wide ditch and large casemated bastions remain today in an unrestored condition (**35**). It is notable as the last of the self-contained bastioned forts to be built in England. To the west, beyond Gosport and

Haslar, was another slightly earlier large bastioned fort. The adjacent Stokes Bay was considered vulnerable to a landing force and Fort Monckton was built here, supplemented by small batteries and entrenchments along the beach. The impressive casemated line of Fort Blockhouse, opposite the Round Tower, was built in the 1820s.

The great period of defensive expansion was in the mid-nineteenth century and brought in the Isle of Wight, which had received little attention since Tudor times. This expansion began as a result of the 1852 invasion 'panic' with a strengthening of the western entrance to the Solent – the Needles Passage. Extra batteries were built outside Henry VIII's Hurst Castle and these were complemented on the Isle of Wight by the building of the newfangled, three-storey casemated Fort Albert, opposite Hurst, and now converted into flats (**36**). A much criticized Fort Victoria, of which only the shell now remains, was also built on the Isle of Wight to the west of Yarmouth. More significant, however, were the five detached and self-contained forts across the promontory, known as the Gosport Advanced Line, well to the west of the town. In terms of military engineering they were also technically advanced, following what was to be known as the 'Prussian' or 'polygonal' school of fortification design. This was a breakaway from the continuous bastioned line which was so extravagant to arm and man and increasingly ineffective, but which had been dominant in defence works for the best part of 300 years. These 'polygonal' forts at Gosport were among the first of their kind to be built in England and they anticipated the type of land fortification adopted in the 1860s. Fort Brockhurst is a fully conserved example with a wide wet moat flanked by large caponiers at the angles of the fort for self-defence, a circular 'keep of last resort' in the gorge and barrack casemates below the ramparts which carried the main armament (**37**, **colour plate 9**). These guns covered the intervals between the forts as well as firing to the front.

The Royal Commission report of 1860 closely analysed the existing defences of Portsmouth and the Solent in the light of changing artillery and

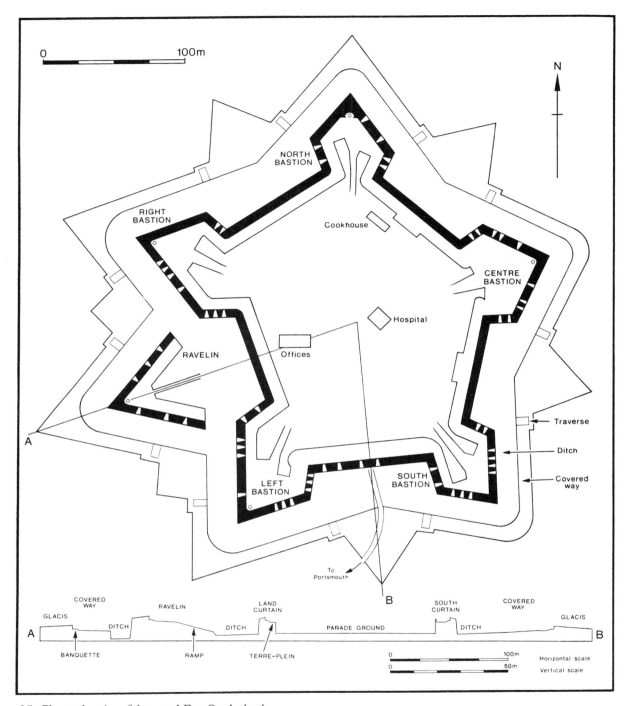

35 *Plan and section of the second Fort Cumberland*
as in c. *1820.*

36 *Fort Albert, Isle of Wight: the rear of the three-storey Fort Albert, built following the 1852 'panic', with World War II twin 6-pounder positions on the roof. Hurst Castle is in the background across the Needles Passage.*

37 *Fort Brockhurst: entrance to keep flanked by two-tiered musketry caponiers.*

38 *Gun-drill with a rifled muzzle loader on a traversing carriage in a new concrete barbette emplacement at Southsea West Battery.*

ship technology and made radical and extensive proposals. The range of the new rifled guns could now achieve 9000yd (over 8km) and were much more accurate. The defences were, therefore, taken much further out to landward, and along the south-east and south-west coasts of the Isle of Wight. In addition, sea-forts were to be constructed upon shoals in the Solent (see **14**). These recommendations, particularly the sea-forts, provoked intense hostility in naval circles as wasteful and unnecessary. There was much public debate, but the scheme was eventually carried out though with considerable modification.

The self-contained Royal Commission forts ('Palmerston's Follies') are conspicuous today along the high ridge of Portsdown to the north of Portsmouth, and in the four sea-forts commanding the eastern entrance to the Solent and its anchorage, supported by the Puckpool Mortar Battery east of Ryde. The old enceinte around Portsmouth and the newer line at Portsea were in effect replaced by the bastioned Hilsea Lines across the top of the island each side of Portsbridge. A new fort at Gilkicker strengthened the western defences, and Southsea Castle to the east had large open batteries added on either side (**38**). On the Isle of Wight the potential landing point at Sandown, protected earlier by Henry VIII, was fortified anew and the eastern batteries had a defensible barracks behind them at Bembridge. On the western side of the island was a cluster of forts and batteries with Golden Hill Fort serving as a defensible barracks. At the Needles itself there was a new fort (see **32**).

Many of the forts are accessible for today's visitors. Forts Widley and Nelson on Portsdown, and Fort Brockhurst on the Gosport Line, are open to the public. These land-forts were intended to forestall a possible land attack in strength striking at Portsmouth from the rear (**39**). The main long-range armament was mounted on top of the earth ramparts, covering the field and capable of enfilading the intervals between the forts. The intervals were also covered by mortar batteries at the angles of the ramparts. The most visible element are the large defensible barracks at the rear of the land-forts. Spitbank Fort, the closest to Portsmouth of the sea-forts, is also open to the public. The most spectacular of the coastal batteries is Hurst Castle where two long, granite-faced, casemated wing batteries, with their embrasures filled with wrought-iron shields, embrace Henry VIII's castle and where rifled muzzle-loader guns have been mounted in two of the casemates (**40, 41**). The Needles Battery on the Isle of Wight is also accessible and has a complex later history.

This mid-nineteenth-century defensive ring, together with the fortifications on the Isle of Wight, was to remain the physical limit of the Portsmouth defences; although the armament and its mountings were to be brought up to date as breech-loading guns replaced the old muzzle loaders shortly before 1900. There was a great reduction in the number of guns in the land-forts around the turn of the century but, shortly before the outbreak of war in 1914, there was a return to the belief in the feasibility of invasion and the Portsdown Line was prepared for infantry defence together with emplacements for heavy field and machine-guns. At sea, the menace of fast torpedo boats was countered by the provision of fighting lights, booms and quick-firers. This adaptation to a new form of sea warfare can be best appreciated at the Needles Battery where there is an extensive deployment of searchlight and fighting-light provision (**42**).

Chatham and Sheerness

Perhaps more than Portsmouth, Chatham had a visible association with the navy in the sixteenth century due to the use of the Medway as a place for the laying up of ships when not on active duty. The emergence of the dockyard, however, was slow. Although the naval presence was established in 1547, Chatham did not acquire a dry

39 *Isometric projection of Fort Southwick, one of the Portsdown line of land-forts of the 1860s. The main armament was mounted on the ramparts with mortar batteries in the forward 'shoulders' of the trace. The ditch is defended by caponiers, and a defensible barracks occupies the gorge.*

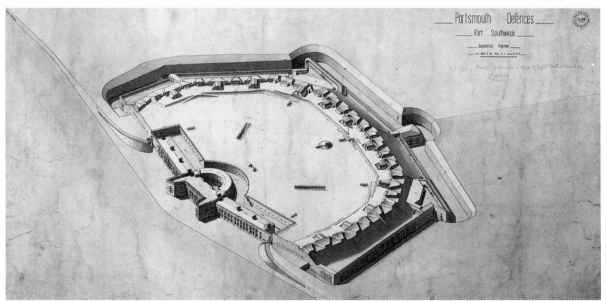

40 *Hurst Castle from the air. Two long casemated batteries of the 1860s were added on either side of the Henrician blockhouse to defend the Needles Passage.*

41 *Cross section of a casemate for a rifled muzzle-loader gun. This is a casemate typical of the 1860 Royal Commission coastal batteries.*

1 *Aerial view of Dover Castle. In the foreground is the Spur with anti-tank blocks at its tip as part of a World War II road-block. Beyond the Castle is the breakwater of the Admiralty Harbour.*

2 The Death of Major
Peirson, 6 January 1781
*by J.S. Copley, 1783. Major
Peirson was largely responsible
for foiling the attempted invasion
of Jersey in 1781 by engaging
the French troops in the Market
Square of St Helier.*

3 *The Armada of 1588.
Engagement of the English and
Spanish fleets between Portland
Bill and the Isle of Wight,
showing the battle off Portland
Bill and then the English fleet
re-formed into four squadrons
off the Isle of Wight.*

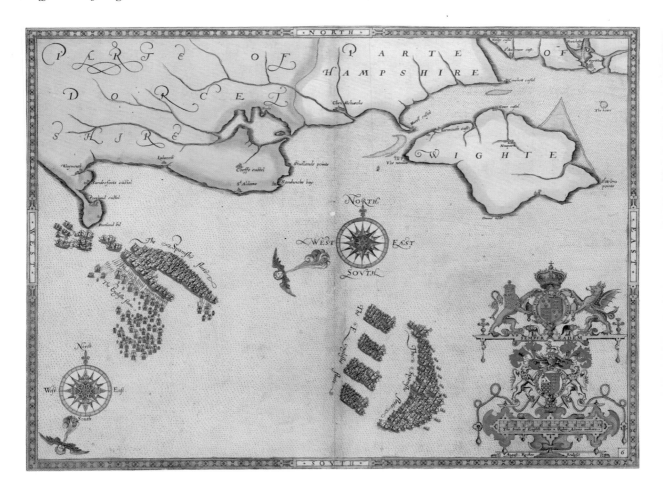

4 Dutch Ships in the Medway
1667 by William Schellinks.

5 Convoy arriving off
St Anthony Lighthouse, Falmouth
*by John Platt. The convoy is passing
through a boom defence. Soldiers are
making their way to a searchlight
position at the bottom left and in the
background is Pendennis Castle.*

6 The Castles in the Downs, *a late seventeenth-century painting of the east Kent castles – Walmer, Deal and, in the distance, Sandown.*

7 *Aerial view of Tilbury Fort. On the riverside are the quick-firer emplacements and two 6-inch gun positions on the re-formed earthworks of the 1870s.*

8 *Aerial view of Pendennis Castle from the south-east showing the Henrician castle enclosed by the late sixteenth-century bastioned enceinte. Half Moon Battery is to the left, and Crab Quay Battery is at the bottom left.*

9 *Aerial view of Fort Brockhurst.*

10 (Opposite, above) *Plymouth: town and Royal Citadel. Sir Bernard de Gomme's plan of the Citadel and panorama of the town, 1672.*

11 (Opposite, below) *Aerial view of Carisbrooke Castle showing the medieval castle enclosed by the late sixteenth-century bastioned enceinte.*

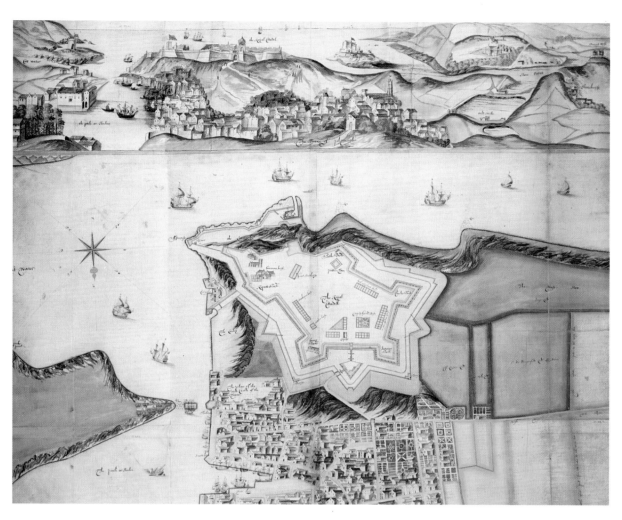

12 *Dover Castle, anti-aircraft gun operations room. Throughout World War II the network of tunnels in the cliff below the castle was used as a command headquarters.*

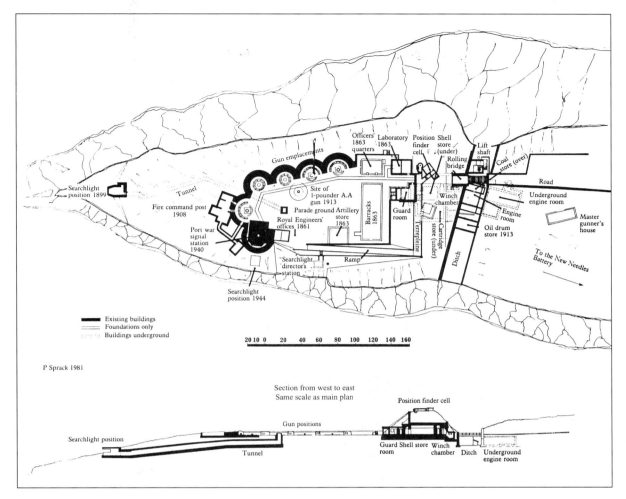

Officers' Laboratory Position Shell Lift
1863 1863 finder store shaft
quarters cell (under)

Gun emplacements Rolling Coal
bridge store (over)

Searchlight Road
position 1899 Tunnel Site of Winch
1-pounder A.A chamber Underground
Fire command post gun 1913 engine room
1908 Parade ground Artillery Guard Engine Master
Royal Engineers' store room room gunner's
Port war offices 1861 1863 house
signal Cartridge Oil drum
station store store 1913
1940 (under)
To the New Needles
Searchlight Ramp Ditch Battery
director's
station

Searchlight
position 1944

▬▬ Existing buildings
⎯⎯ Foundations only
⋯⋯ Buildings underground

20 10 0   20   40   60   80   100   120   140   160

P Sprack 1981

Section from west to east
Same scale as main plan

Position finder cell

Gun positions

Searchlight position

Guard Shell store Winch
Tunnel room chamber Ditch Underground
engine room

dock until early in the seventeenth century. Upnor Castle (described earlier) remained the principal fort until the Dutch raid of 1667 proved the weakness of the Medway defences as a whole (see **colour plate 4**).

With the customary hurry to close the stable door after the event, new defences were commissioned and designed by Sir Bernard de Gomme. Emphasis was given to Sheerness where a fort, under construction in 1667, had been burnt by the Dutch. A new fort at Sheerness coincided with the construction of a dockyard facing the Netherlands and the North Sea. The defences of Harwich and its dockyard were also improved at the same time because of the Dutch menace. Covering the approaches to Chatham, and replacing the now redundant Upnor Castle,

42 *Plan and cross-section of the Old Needles Battery showing gun emplacements and searchlight positions.*

which became a gunpowder supply store, were the two powerful batteries, Gillingham and Cockham Wood already mentioned. At Sheerness, towards the Point and on the seaward side where it has not been obliterated by the new ferry terminal, is the Portland stone face of the scarp and the corbels of a sentinel house of de Gomme's fort, which with its simple ravelin and bastion front had enclosed the new dockyard (see **43**).

Chatham Dockyard itself was not made defensible until a simple bastion trace was constructed in the middle of the eighteenth century. The ditch and rampart, regularly flanked by projecting bastions, runs along the high ground to the south enclosing the village of Brompton, so that they are often referred to as the Brompton Lines. At the end of the eighteenth century both ends of the lines had been substantially retrenched around two rectangular redoubts – Amherst and Townshend – and given elaborate additional works. That towards the town has escaped destruction by the Victorian steam-dockyard development, which engulfed the eastern end of the lines, and is known today as Fort Amherst. This is a spectacular piece of fortification which is in the process of being rescued from dereliction and restored. It overlooks the town of Chatham. The chalk cliff is tunnelled for communication passages, and cut by wide brick-revetted ditches, which are flanked by gun positions and fortified barracks.

Rochester Bridge was a strategic crossing point of the Medway on the line of the main road from Dover to London. For this reason it formed part of the counter-invasion plans of the Napoleonic Wars, and forts and gun towers were built on the heights above Rochester at that time. The newer works were associated with the Brompton Lines to form a defensive ring facing south (discussed in the following chapter).

Sheerness Dockyard meanwhile developed in its own right during the eighteenth century. In the 1780s a new bastioned envelope enclosed the expanded dockyard and the associated Blue Town beyond the seventeenth century lines, which contained dockyard workers' housing much in the same way as occurred at Plymouth Dock and Portsea (43). The complete enceinte survived until the late 1960s as the last English town, other than Berwick-upon-Tweed, to retain its complete bastioned trace but it fell victim to attempts for economic regeneration of the area following the rundown of the dockyard.

Sheerness and the Medway defences were vastly expanded as a result of the 1860 Royal Commission report (see 59). A massive, two-tiered casemated fort was built at Garrison Point at the entrance to the Medway on the site of Henry VIII's blockhouse (44). A Martello-type gun tower had earlier been built in the 1840s opposite

Sheerness on Grain Spit and this, after 1860, was backed up by powerful batteries and defensible barracks on the Isle of Grain itself. The defences of the Medway were linked by means of Slough Fort, near Allhallows on the Isle of Grain, with the new forts of Coalhouse, Cliffe and Shornemead around the Lower Hope in the Thames Estuary which were constructed well in advance of the earlier defence line between Tilbury and Gravesend. To the south of Sheerness yet another line consisting of a wide ditch and rampart was dug, the Queenborough Lines, which protected the landward approach. This was intended to be secured by a tower prepared to receive an iron turret for two guns but this did not materialize. Much of the waterfilled ditch does, however, remain.

Garrison Point Fort of the 1860s has recently been converted to a ferry terminal. Few internal details remain but the massive bulk of this two-tiered fort can be appreciated. Only two such two-storey casemated forts were built in England; the other, now more seriously mutilated, is at Picklecombe on the Cornish side of Plymouth Sound. Controlling the mouth of the estuary in front of Garrison Point was a Brennan torpedo station, an example of the defensive use of the controlled torpedo which was adopted late in the nineteenth century (see 17). Near the Grain tower are remains of the boom defence of the First World War, which controlled access to the Medway, but the batteries and defensible barracks of Grain Fort have been removed.

The 1860 Royal Commission report recommended a ring of land-forts to the south of Chatham similar to those of Portsmouth and Plymouth. In the event these were omitted on the grounds of cost. However, the land had already been bought and an ingeneous solution was found by the engineers during the 1870s. The Director of Convict Prisons was Major-General Sir E.F. Du Cane, who had previously designed

43 *Map of Sheerness with the plan of the bastioned front of de Gomme's late seventeenth-century fortifications at the tip of the promontory and Blue Town enclosed by a late eighteenth-century trace.*

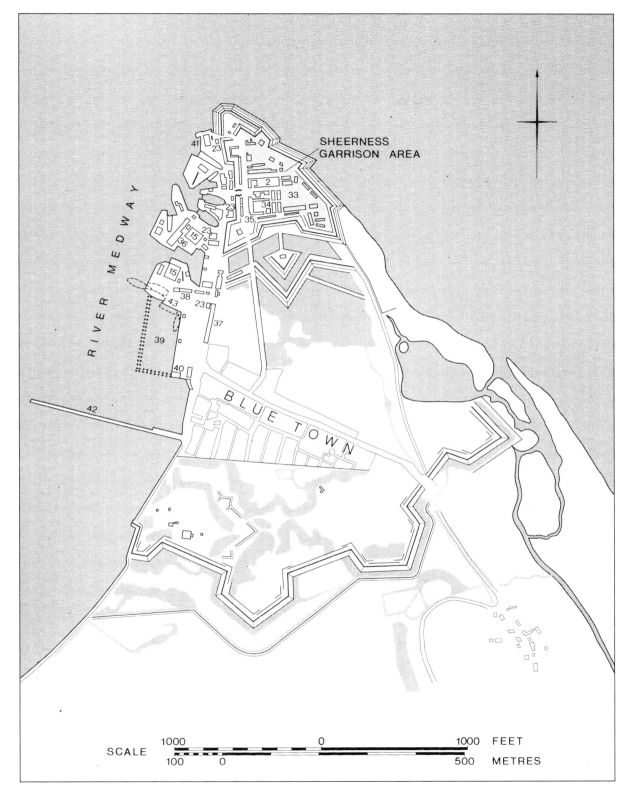

SHEERNESS GARRISON AREA

RIVER MEDWAY

BLUE TOWN

SCALE

1000   0   1000   FEET

100   0   500   METRES

44 *Garrison Point Fort, Sheerness. Two-tiered casemated fort of the 1860s with a characteristic Sheppey machine-gun position of World War I below, guarding the end of the boom across the Medway.*

the Commission forts at Dover and the land-forts at Plymouth. He saw to it that a new prison was built at Borstal, south-east of Chatham, in 1875, and it was prison labour which built Fort Borstal alongside. The eventual construction of the crescent of forts south and east of Chatham was to take more than twenty years. During that time the form and function of fixed land defences were to evolve rapidly. They were to become much more earthwork infantry redoubts, with the artillery detached and placed in concealed and increasingly mobile positions.

Plymouth

The early defences of Plymouth had been centred on the Hoe and on Drake's (formerly St Nicholas) Island and, even during the seventeenth century, the newly built Royal Citadel, with the slightly earlier gun tower at Mount Batten, defended the entrance to the Cattewater and the traditional harbour of Sutton Pool. Standing on the ramparts of the Citadel and looking out to sea, not only are these immediate defences apparent but stretching out beyond Drake's Island are the two successive defence lines of the 1860s and that of the late nineteenth century. De Gomme's Royal Citadel is a magnificent monument to late seventeenth-century engineering, its irregular bastioned enceinte making the best of a difficult site and subsuming parts of its late sixteenth-century predecessor (**colour plate 10**). Some of the internal buildings survive at least externally and its glory is the fine baroque main gate. What the Citadel lacks today are its outworks. Only the ghost of its ravelin and the rock-cut ditch survive; the road and municipal gardening have destroyed the covered way. This was as much a fortress to dominate the town as a defence of the harbour. The town had held out for Parliament for the whole of the Civil War and, as at Hull, this tenacity was not forgotten at the Restoration in 1660.

The naval base at Plymouth was a comparatively late creation, reflecting the increasing importance of the Atlantic and the western approaches to the Channel to naval strategy. In 1689 the Admiralty wrote to the Navy Board asking it to consider the possibility of building a dock at Plymouth. This was to be a small dock 'for cruising ships only'. The site chosen was the 'Ham Oze', well to the west of Plymouth itself, at the mouth of the Tamar. In 1692 a formal decision was taken to create a full-scale dockyard. In 1746 Admirals Anson and Warren advocated that in future the Western Squadron should be refitted at Plymouth. Plymouth Dock, or simply Dock, and its attendant town and naval-supply facilities therefore grew up separately from Plymouth itself. The Royal William Victualling Yard was built at Stonehouse in 1826–35 and the North Yard of 1848 catered for the Victorian steam navy. Dock was only renamed as Devonport in 1824.

From the start, the defences of the dockyard were negligible. Already in existence were the sixteenth-century blockhouses at Devil's Point (**45**) and on the shore at Mount Edgcumbe at the entrance to the Tamar. Distinct from the dockyard wall, the highly irregular bastioned earthwork trace enclosing the whole of the dockyard and town complex was not begun until 1756. The lines were of a slight nature mounting only 30 guns. In the parliamentary debates on dockyard defences in the 1770s it was said that 'the construction of the lines is not calculated to resist a regular siege', which was putting the position politely. In 1779 improvements were proposed and carried out but little of these curtains and bastions remains today. A more serious weakness lay beyond, since Dock and its fortified lines could be commanded from high ground in many places to the north and east, and an enemy landing to the west, on the Cornish side of the Tamar, could bombard and completely control it.

45 *Devil's Point Blockhouse, Plymouth, of c. 1500, covering the mouth of the Tamar at Western King.*

46 *A redoubt at the northern end of the line on Maker Heights, Cornwall.*

This led to the construction of detached redoubts to command the three hills in the immediate vicinity of Dock: Mount Pleasant, Mount Wise and Stonehouse Hill, and new batteries were built along the water's edge at Western King and Passage Point. The anticipated French landing point was Cawsand Bay on the Cornish side, which was covered by redoubts sited on the foreshore. In the 1780s, as a result of the initiative of the Duke of Richmond, comparable defensive improvements to those at Portsmouth were made. A large tract of the Maker Heights on the Cornish side was bought in 1784 and five detached earthwork redoubts were later thrown up across the peninsula. They were permanent works with masonry revetted scarps and deep ditches, but essentially batteries with only a minimum provision for self-defence in the form of a drawbridge and a loopholed gorge wall (**46**). By 1804 a barracks had been built for the men manning them.

As at other places, the continuing need to extend the defences of the dockyard and its associated installations saw an expansion in the mid-nineteenth century (**47**). The outward growth of the defences of the Sound can be seen in three broad chronological stages: the first and inner line from Western King, Drake's Island to the Hoe and Mount Batten of the sixteenth and seventeenth centuries; Picklecombe, the Breakwater and

Staddon/Bovisand in the middle of the nineteenth century; and the outer line of Penlee Point and Renney Rocks by the turn of the twentieth century.

Expansion came first on the western side of the Sound at Picklecombe Point in the 1840s and then at Staddon Point opposite. The defences of Plymouth as a whole were reviewed in 1858 when recommendations were made for massive three-tier casemated batteries replacing the forward defences of ten years previous, and casemated batteries at either end of the recently built breakwater (1812–47) with more guns mounted on Drake's Island. The possibility of hostile landings in Cawsand and Whitesand Bays in Cornwall led to the provision of an advanced defence line in front of Anthony with land-forts on either flank at Tregantle and Scraesdon along with additional coastal batteries. At Tregantle the extensive fort had a ditched 'keep' to the rear and Scraesdon also shared similarities with the forts of the Gosport Advanced Line. There was also thought to be a need for a line of detached forts and batteries along the high ground north and east of Plymouth between St Budeaux and Staddon in advance of the inner enceinte represented by the old Devonport Lines.

The Anthony Advanced Position was begun right away, and when the Defence Commission reported in 1860, some of these earlier proposals were approved and additional suggestions recommended. Plymouth was regarded by the Commissioners as the second great naval arsenal and port after Portsmouth. Its sea defences embraced three objectives:

> the defence of the entrance to the Hamoaze, the security of the Sound as an anchorage for our own ships and against its occupation by an enemy, and the adoption of means to prevent the bombardment of the dockyard at long range.

As at Portsmouth, land defences were considered vital. The north-eastern defences required an advanced line of detached works, its left resting on the Tamar near St Budeaux, and its right at

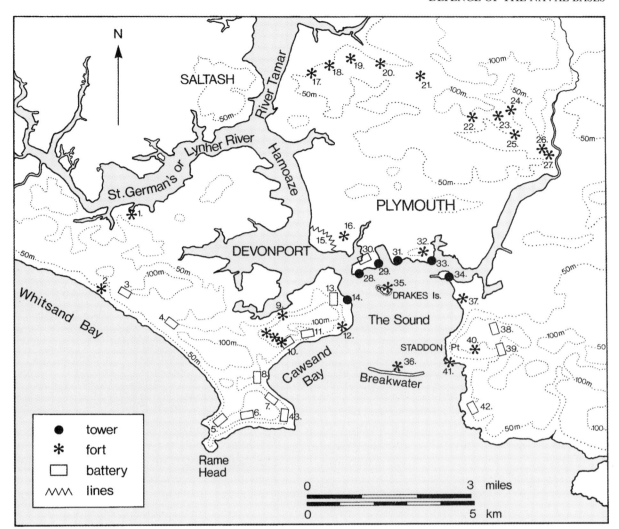

47 *Map of Plymouth and Devonport defences: 1 Scraesdon Fort; 2 Tregantle Fort; 3 Tregantle Down Battery; 4 Whitesand Bay Battery; 5 Polhawn Battery; 6 Rame Church Battery; 7 Pier Cellars Battery; 8 Cawsand Battery; 9 Maker Heights Redoubts; 10 Grenville Battery; 11 Hawkin's Battery; 12 Picklecombe Fort; 13 Garden Battery; 14 Barnpool or Mount Edgcumbe Tower; 15 Devonport Lines; 16 Mount Wise Redoubt; 17 Ernesettle Fort; 18 Agaton Fort; 19 Knowles Battery; 20 Woodlands Fort; 21 Crownhill Fort; 22 Bowden Fort;* *23 Egg Buckland Keep; 24 Forder Battery; 25 Austin Fort; 26 Fort Efford; 27 Laira Battery; 28 Devil's Point Blockhouse; 29 Firestone Bay Blockhouse; 30 Western King Battery; 31 Hoe blockhouses; 32 Plymouth Citadel; 33 Fisher's Nose Tower; 34 Mount Batten Tower; 35 Drake's (St Nicholas) Island; 36 Breakwater Fort; 37 Fort Stamford; 38 Twelve Acre Brake and Watch House Batteries; 39 Brownhill Battery; 40 Fort Staddon; 41 Fort Bovisand and Staddon Point Battery; 42 Renney and Lentney Batteries; 43 Penlee Point Battery.*

Catdown above the Cattewater. These forts replaced the old Devonport Lines whose existence was said to be desirable but impracticable. Additional batteries were needed to command the

Sound, and behind the Breakwater was built a new iron sea-fort similar to those in the Solent (see **13**).

In the centre of the North-Eastern Line, and the hub on which it turned, is Crownhill Fort,

48 *Aerial view of Crownhill Fort, Plymouth. The key to the north-east position in Plymouth's land defences.*

now preserved by the Landmark Trust (**48**). It had remained in military occupation until the late 1970s and was not vandalized. Not only are its internal barracks, officers' mess, store buildings and magazines intact but the massive earthwork defences have been cleared of vegetation so that the manner by which the fort could protect itself by means of flanking defences in the ditch from masonry two-tiered caponiers, can be clearly seen.

The great two-tiered casemated battery at Picklecombe has been drastically converted into an exclusive hotel. The matching single-storey casemated battery with iron shields similar to those at Hurst Castle is at Bovisand on the Devon side. It is intact and used as an underwater training centre but accessible.

Later in the nineteenth century, as the range and sheer fire-power of warships increased, it was necessary to push the coastal batteries further out

to the very opening of the Sound (**49**). Following the Stanhope Report in 1891, the coast defences were modernized with emphasis at Plymouth on the need to cover Whitesand Bay from which it was anticipated that warships could stand off and shell the dockyard. Drake's Island and Pier Cellars had been equipped to launch Brennan torpedoes, and 6-pounder quick-firing guns were mounted at Picklecombe, Breakwater Fort and Bovisand to cover the underwater minefields. In the decade before the First World War, the old rifled muzzle-loading guns installed in the 1880s were replaced with medium- and long-range breech-loading guns together with quick-firing batteries to combat fast torpedo boats. Batteries for long-range, 9.2-inch guns were emplaced at Renney (near Wembury) and Penlee Point.

49 *Aerial view of the late nineteenth-century Maker and Grenville Batteries for 12.5-inch rifled muzzle loaders overlooking Cawsand Bay, Cornwall, with Cawsand Battery behind the village.*

4

Invasion coasts

The direct threat of invasion was met in three ways. The navy, as we have seen, was the first line of defence; the home defence forces of the regular army, the militia and volunteers were there should the navy fail to control the Channel; and various defensive positions, permanent fortifications or emergency fieldworks, were to be the third element.

Permanent defences of strategic places such as naval bases could be planned and constructed over a long timespan but the immediate risk of landings on open beaches and a rapid enemy advance inland could happen almost anywhere. The government's dilemma was always whether to meet an invading army once it had landed with a counter-attack from a mobile field force, or attempt to predict the most likely landing places and fight the invaders on the beaches from prepared positions. By their nature, invasion crises arose quickly and demanded emergency action. Defences in such circumstances were inevitably earthworks of a temporary nature: trenches, breastworks and batteries thrown up over the space of a few weeks and days. In time these leave little surface trace. More permanent anti-invasion measures are less common and survive mainly as Martello towers, concrete pillboxes and emergency batteries whether of Napoleonic vintage or from 1940.

Counter-measures against invasion range further than just beach fortification. From medieval times, watches were kept along the coasts and an early-warning network of fire beacons estab-lished. The Tudor beacons are well documented (**50**). Rather more informative signalling systems developed in the eighteenth and nineteenth centuries. In the twentieth century, radio-direction finding, sound mirrors, radar and Royal Observer Corps posts provided early warning of attack from air and sea. Directly involved in home defence were those outside the ranks of the regular army: the militia, volunteers, Sea Fencibles, Home Guard and Civil Defence. In addition to the defences built and paid for by the government were those erected on local initiative by individual landowners or communities.

There were four main critical periods in the country's history which have left visible remains of anti-invasion works along the Channel coast: the combined French and Spanish threat of 1539; the Armada of 1588 and subsequent Spanish activity; the danger of French invasion from 1790

50 *Sixteenth-century warning beacons in Dorset.*

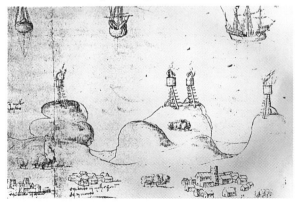

onwards and especially the Napoleonic threat of 1803–15; and Operation 'Sealion' in 1940. Henry VIII's response to the first of the threats has been largely covered above and the defence works of 1940 are described in the final chapter.

These four periods of particular peril and the responses to them reflect significant changes in defence technology. Henry VIII's 'castles' mark the transition of medieval forms as they came to terms with the inevitability of gunpowder artillery. The Armada period demonstrates the establishment of a conventional bastion system of all-round defence based on Italian prototypes, which had barely impinged on the castles and blockhouses of Henry VIII. By the time of the Napoleonic Wars, the bastion system, which had reached its apogee at the end of the seventeenth century under the influence of the engineers Vauban and Coehoorn, had become less satisfactory. Its development had either stagnated or had moved to ever greater complexity and extravagance. Marshal de Saxe, in the middle of the eighteenth century, was sceptical of elaborate defences around towns and claimed that it would be more sensible to set the army entrenching strategic points in open country. During the latter half of the eighteenth century, engineers across Europe began to adapt fortification to suit particular circumstances and believed that improvised fieldworks were a valid alternative to complex permanent fortification. The formulation of radical change came principally from the Marquis de Montalembert whose first volume of *La Fortification perpendiculaire* was published in 1776. For coastal defence he advocated high, multi-tiered towers with large numbers of guns in bombproof casemates able to deliver a great weight of fire over a short space of time

The effect of these ideas can be seen in some of the British works of the 1770s and 1780s. The use of towers in the Channel Islands, detached redoubts on Maker Heights, the increasing use of casemates and caponiers at Fort Cumberland and Fort Monckton on either side of Portsmouth, and the later three-tiered coastal gun tower of Fort Albert, Isle of Wight (see **36**), show that British

engineers were aware that the traditional bastion system could be improved. This ability to change and keep up with new trends developed more emphatically during the programme of coastal defences stimulated by the threat of Napoleonic invasion until it seemed that everything was dominated by the Martello tower and its derivatives.

By the twentieth century, a revolution in the nature of fixed defences contrasted the reinforced concrete bunker and armoured turret with the infantry trench and redoubt together with mobile artillery. The combination of the dive-bomber and the tank produced *blitzkrieg*. This greater mobility of warfare in 1940 required defensive measures of a new and different kind.

Spanish armadas

Reports of Philip II's preparations for an invasion had been brought to the Privy Council as early as 1584. Defence planning was therefore a key preoccupation of Elizabethan government throughout the 1580s and detailed orders concerning defence arrangements in the maritime counties increasingly flowed from London. They were not before time since there existed only the neglected legacy of the castles and blockhouses from the 1540s and early 1550s, out of date and run down in garrisons and ordnance. The main defence expenditure was first concentrated on the Isle of Wight at Carisbrooke Castle, and at Portsmouth, where the embryonic bastioned defences of Henry VIII were brought up to contemporary standards.

By 1587–8, Philip's intentions were apparent – a seaborne force from Spain in combination with the army of Flanders – with the focus of operations on the south-east corner of England, but with the possibility of landings anywhere along the south coast. Plymouth was considered a likely objective because of the Spanish need to capture one good harbour close to Spain. Falmouth was already protected by Pendennis and St Mawes Castles but Plymouth had only a line of small blockhouses at the water's edge below the Hoe (**51**), and a small and obsolete castle, and guns on St Nicholas Island.

Preparations along the coasts were hurried and temporary in nature, resembling those dug and erected by the inhabitants of harbour towns in that earlier crisis of 1539. The Privy Council gave instructions to build sconces, trenches and parapets, and to dig pits and drive in stakes on the sea-coasts to impede the landing of the enemy. The stakes were to protrude 8–10in (20–5cm) above the ground surface, thereby deterring troops and horses. Roads were to be obstructed by felling large trees across them and men were to lie in ambush at these obstacles. Shooting practice was to take place weekly for the militia, and carts and horses were to be made perpetually ready for the speedy deployment of munitions, men and field artillery.

The renewal of the traditional beacon system to warn of hostile shipping is well documented in Kent, Hampshire and Dorset. There are illustrations of the beacons themselves as well as the sites and the lines of intercommunication but actual survivals of fire baskets are now absent.

51 *Part of a map of* c. *1540 showing the blockhouses at Plymouth and Stonehouse.*

The Kentish system was based on the beacon at Fairlight, near Hastings (**52**). The beacons were complemented by a postal service carried by horsemen or in small fast ships. The general success of these measures can be judged by the extent of the mobilization in 1588 which has been claimed to have involved about 76,000 men.

The partially trained militia provided a mobile force of about 29,000 which was ordered to operate through the maritime counties and to shadow the Armada as it sailed up the Channel. Special arrangements were made to give mutual aid between these counties. The quality of the militia, however, was not high. Trained bands had been fostered since 1573 but most were untrained, though there was some limited stiffening from professional soldiers who had returned from service in the Netherlands. Some cannon together with powder, match and shot were allocated and in 1587 each of the six front-line counties was meant to receive two cast-iron sakers, two minions and two falcons, together with the appropriate carriages and accessories. A mid-sixteenth-century 'parish gun' from an earlier provision is preserved in Carisbrooke Castle.

Despite the attention given to militia and local defence forces, the government had long been conscious of the weakness of the long coastline and the vulnerability of the major ports. Able but untrained men were drafted to Falmouth, Plymouth, the Sussex coast, Sheppey, Poole, Portsmouth and elsewhere. A list of the 'dangerous places' and those 'fittest to be putt in defence to hinder th'enemye' was drawn up for Kent. Sheppey and Thanet, and the area designated as the Downs, were considered particularly vulnerable. A field force was allocated to the Downs, encamped at Northbourne behind the three Henrician castles of Deal, Sandown and Walmer, and Dover Castle.

The hurriedly constructed sconces, trenches and road-blocks of the time were soon obliterated once danger had passed. Perhaps one of the few examples is a slight earthwork just to the west of

the medieval castle but within the Roman fort of Pevensey. It is a short length of bank with demi-bastions at either end. Two Elizabethan demi culverins were found in the vicinity, one of which has been mounted on a reconstructed field carriage of the period and is to be seen in the castle.

Besides being a possible Spanish objective, Plymouth served as a base for the English fleet which harassed the Spanish Armada. Spending on fortifications there was largely a local responsibility and concerned repairs to the castle, the cost of maintaining the defences and garrison on St Nicholas Island, the building and maintenance of a 'watch house' on Plymouth Hoe, the building of bulwarks, purchase of ordnance and powder, match and shot, the building and repair of gun carriages, and spending on the hire of spy boats and posthorse messengers.

Reference to spending on bulwarks at Plymouth begins in 1585. They were essentially of earthwork and timber. Sir Richard Grenville

52 *Map of the Kent Armada beacons as they were approved by the Lord Lieutenant in 1588 when the Spanish invasion was expected (William Lambarde).*

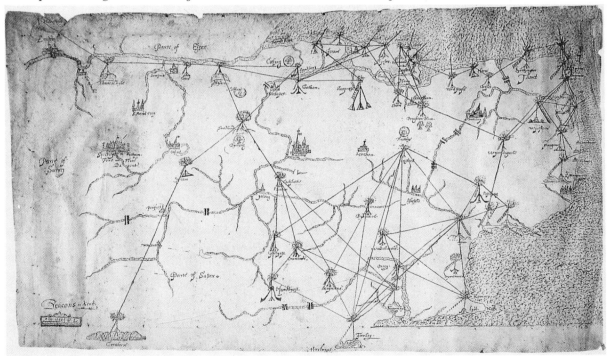

was appointed in 1587 to survey the defences of the south-west coasts and a coloured map is almost certainly associated with his work showing all the blockhouses along the water's edge of Plymouth Hoe. Additional batteries were recommended and the map shows where extra ordnance and militia forces ought to be deployed to defend landing places towards the mouth of the Sound.

The hub of the anti-invasion measures turned on the encampment for the main military forces under the Earl of Leicester at West Tilbury. The army was held on the Essex side of the main Thames river-crossing between Tilbury and Gravesend so that it could move against a Spanish landing whether it came north or south of the river. The West Tilbury Blockhouse, below the site of the camp near the church, was reinforced by an elaborate outer earthwork designed by the Italian engineer Federigo Genebelli, who served the government as a technical adviser (**53**). Its site is now beneath the late seventeenth-century Tilbury Fort.

In the event there was no juncture between Parma's veterans from the Netherlands and the Armada itself, no landings occurred, and the great fleet was dispersed. Yet it was realized that this was not the end of the danger and further attacks were expected. Some lessons had been learnt. At one stage of the Armada's progress up the Channel a landing on the Isle of Wight was anticipated which, if it had succeeded, would

53 *Plan of West Tilbury Blockhouse enclosed by the Armada-period earthworks designed by the Italian consultant military engineer Genebelli.*

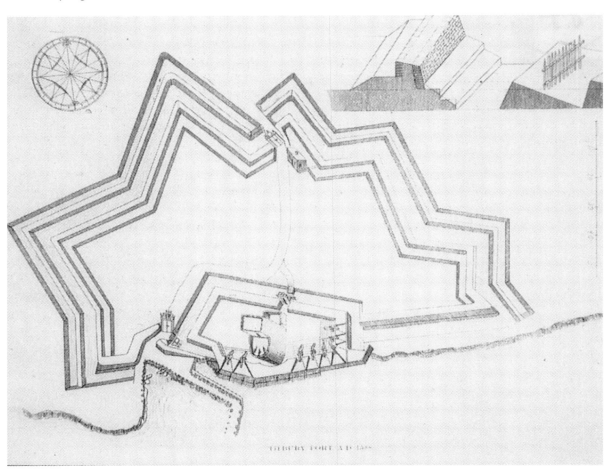

have neutralized the key naval base of Portsmouth. Carisbrooke Castle in the centre of the island was therefore considerably improved. Its medieval walls and towers were no longer a match against gunpowder artillery but two ravelins had already been added in 1586–7 and two of its mural towers were remodelled into shallow angle bastions and named 'knights', or more conventionally, 'cavaliers'. Then in 1597–1601 the castle was enclosed by a new enceinte flanked by Italian-style orillon bastions and with a covered way on the counterscarp (**colour plate 11**). An unusual feature at this date is an earthwork tenaille in the ditch to protect the faces of the curtains. These new works were also designed by Genebelli and illustrate the fundamental change that had overtaken the defence of the medieval castle.

After 1588 there was a shift of defensive emphasis westwards. The vulnerability of Plymouth was recognized and a self-contained fort was begun on the Hoe in 1593 to the design of the English engineer Robert Adams, though it was later adapted and completed by its first captain, Sir Ferdinando Gorges.

The extreme south-west of Cornwall suffered from Spanish raids as well as the threat of large-scale invasion especially when it was learnt that there was a scheme to capture Falmouth. This led to the fortification of the Pendennis headland as a whole in 1598, bringing the Henrician castle within a new bastioned enclosure (see **colour plate 8**). Not far away at St Ives are bastioned earthworks, faced with granite boulders, defending the Island above the harbour. There are references in the borough records which suggest that these were built in the 1590s and, if so, they represent the best-preserved Elizabethan local earthwork defences against Spanish raid or invasion.

In 1593 Robert Adams, who had been partly responsible for designing Plymouth Fort, built Star Castle on the Hugh above St Mary's in the Isles of Scilly to control the harbour there (**54**). It was little more than a blockhouse with the trace of an eight-pointed star. The Channel Islands were also strengthened with the remodelling of

54 Star Castle, St Mary's, Isles of Scilly, built in 1593.

Castle Cornet in Guernsey and the effective replacement of Mont Orgueil on Jersey by the new Elizabeth Castle (**55**).

These fortifications were intended as permanent works and have all survived apart from Plymouth Fort; although even here the seventeenth-century replacement, the Royal Citadel, incorporates some of its seaward lines. They represent the establishment of the bastion system of fortification in England and its local development. The Carisbrooke Castle enceinte is somewhat old-fashioned; its long curtains probably could not have been defended adequately by contemporary musketry with its limited range, or from the guns in the restricted flankers behind the orillons. The trace of the new works at Pendennis, while necessarily irregular because it had to be adapted to a narrow elongated promontory, showed design improvements which reflected the changes in military engineering then being developed in the Low Countries. Here the designer was the English military engineer Paul Ive, who had also built the new Elizabeth Castle on Jersey.

Martello towers

The most prolonged and intense period of danger from an invasion force camped on the opposite side of the Channel came from Napoleonic France during the years 1801–5. The response from government was, unusually, to plan an extended

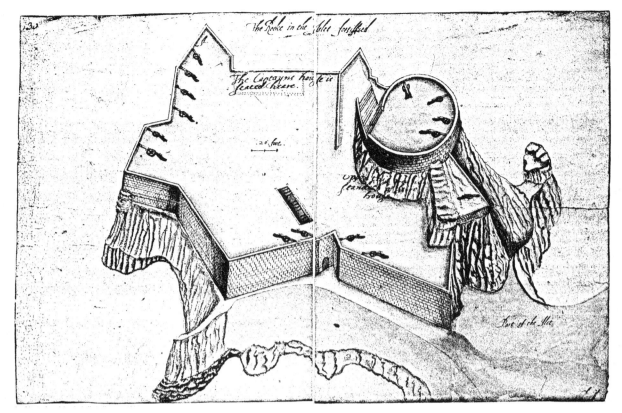

55 *Elizabeth Castle, Jersey, as designed by Paul Ive in 1594.*

defence of the coastline and the anticipated invasion beaches (see **6**). The likely nature of the attack, its direction and immediate objectives were known to the British government through the defection in 1793 of General Dumouriez, who had himself plotted an earlier project to invade England. A comprehensive report on the state of the country's defences was prepared as early as 1794.

Just as the French had a well-matured range of plans for invasion and strategies for advancing towards London once on English soil, so there were British defensive schemes of long standing. Some were even published, such as Colonel George Hanger's *Reflections on the Menaced Invasion and the means of protecting The Capital by preventing the enemy from landing in any part contiguous to it* (1804). The man who had the most practical responsibility for defensive preparations in south-east

England was the Quartermaster-General of the Forces from 1796 to 1803 and Commander of the Southern District from 1803 to 1805, General Sir David Dundas.

From the second half of the eighteenth century there were many batteries along the coasts wherever there was a harbour however small, from the Firth of Forth right round to the Bristol Channel to Fishguard and up to the Mersey and Workington. Along the Channel coast, away from the main concentrations of fire-power, there were minor batteries at Whitstable, Margate, Ramsgate and Pegwell Bay. South of the three castles of the Downs were three 32-pounders at St Margaret's Bay. Moving west beyond Dover there were two batteries at Folkestone (one at Copt Point and one at East Wear), Sandgate Castle and Shorncliffe, and three batteries at Hythe, each dignified by the title of 'fort' and named after Twiss, Sutherland and Moncrieff, with a smaller work on Saltwood Heights. Hythe was a military centre of considerable importance at this time. There was a battery at Lympne, New Romney and Dymchurch Sluice, a redoubt and four batteries at Dungeness and a battery at Lydd. The Sussex coast had ten batteries: Rye, Hastings, two at Langney Point, Eastbourne, Seaford, Blatchington, Newhaven, Brighton and Arundel Haven.

West of the concentration of defences around Portsmouth, the Solent and the Isle of Wight, the Henrician castle still covered the harbour of Portland together with some later batteries. Swanage and Bridport had three guns each. Into Devon, Seaton had a few guns but the Berry Head batteries above Brixham, and the battery at Dartmouth, were well equipped. West of Plymouth and excluding the Falmouth fortress, the minor harbours of Looe, Fowey, Charlestown, Mevagissey, Mount's Bay, St Ives, Portreath and Padstow and up to Ilfracombe in north Devon all had their batteries. The calibre of the armament varied enormously at all these locations. The most frequently mounted pieces were 24-pounders followed by 32-pounders.

Many of the long-established fortresses were augmented by additional batteries. The newly improved Thames defences at Tilbury Fort and New Tavern Fort, Gravesend, were strengthened by advanced batteries downstream. These batteries were semicircular in plan, having a wide rampart with guns mounted on traversing platforms behind. A triangular-shaped area to the rear enclosed by a brick wall contained weatherboarded barrack buildings and a magazine. Likewise at Hurst Castle, controlling the Needles Passage, two six-gun batteries were sited on the shingle bank outside the castle early in 1795, to augment the limited number of guns on the old-fashioned semicircular bastions. Like many batteries of the time, they were each to have a shot-heating furnace; red-hot shot being a potent weapon against wooden ships. By 1803 more work was carried out at Hurst which entailed inserting a vault in the central tower in order to mount heavy guns on the top. The central tower of Sandgate Castle was similarly converted into a substantial gun tower between 1805 and 1808.

Many of the batteries erected at this time of emergency were of a temporary and simple nature. The guns were protected by a rampart of earth but often were mounted to fire over it, *en barbette*. Unless the batteries were adjuncts of a substantial fortification they were enclosed at the rear, usually by stone or brick walls meeting at a salient angle. The larger batteries in Hythe Bay also followed much the same arrangement but the four at Dungeness were more ambitious. They were roughly hexagonal in shape with barracks and magazine to the rear, enclosed by a loopholed wall flanked by two square, loopholed, two-storeyed bastions. There was accommodation for as many as three officers and fifty men. That at Lade, Denge Beach, is the best survivor due to its occupation by the coast-guards.

Any invasion with London and the seat of government as its objective was predicted to occur between the Thames Estuary and the Isle of Wight. The most vulnerable locations were defined as East Wear Bay near Folkestone, Hythe Bay, and on either side of Dungeness, depending on whether the wind was westerly or easterly. Further west were the beaches near Rye, Pevensey Bay and Eastbourne. West of Beachy Head, Seaford was considered suitable for a landing as were the beaches of Brighton and Hove. General Dundas took the view that because of the lie of the North and South Downs, the French would encounter fewer obstacles the further east they were. Canterbury, he thought, was the key to this approach, although it could mean the invader taking a chance and leaving the fortress of Dover untaken in his rear.

In 1803 there were only some 60,000 men of the regular army stationed in England and 50,000 militia. To these could be added large numbers of ill-trained if enthusiastic Volunteers and Sea Fencibles. There was also an established signalling system linking the south coast with the Admiralty in London and the traditional early-warning system of beacons (see **12**).

It had long been accepted that an enemy could not be prevented from landing, and if he did, the local population was to adopt a 'scorched earth' policy, for example by flooding Romney Marshes. There were practical objections to this latter course. The presence of a very obvious invasion army across the Channel in 1803 required a new strategy. This envisaged preparations against an actual landing combined with defence in depth. The objective was to contain the landing force until the field army could counter-attack, or provide lines of defence in commanding positions well to the rear. Of all these defensive preparations the most visible and characteristic survivals are the Martello towers but, as with the pillbox of 1940, they were only one element of a wider defensive system (**56**).

The towers themselves were a development from those built to defend beaches in the Channel Islands about twenty years before. Tower defence was further stimulated by descriptions of the effective deployment of a gun tower at Cape Mortella in Corsica against a British naval squadron in 1794. It was an action which was to give its name to this particular type of defensive work. In 1797 Sir David Dundas, who had commanded in Corsica at the time of the frustrated naval action at Cape Mortella, proposed in a memorandum on coast defence the desirability of 'disconcerting' an enemy fleet while still at anchor, of preventing him from settling in any roadstead, and of delaying his

landing for twenty-four or forty-eight hours. He favoured the construction of:

> strong, stone towers, favourably situated, not commanded, mounting two or three large guns and protecting, as long as proper, an outward battery of two or more guns, bomb-proof, garrisoned by about thirty men, about 30 feet in height and 12 of interior diameter, entered by a ladder . . . [they] would answer this purpose better than larger batteries and expensive low works. Supposing such a tower to cost £700, one hundred of them properly disposed in the different bays most inviting to an enemy would give great security to a very extensive range of coast.

The idea was given support in a memorandum from a Major Reynolds the following year. Reynolds, having observed the ineffectiveness of the south-coast defences, listed sites for 143 'Martella Towers' between Littlehampton and Yarmouth. Of these he considered 73 urgently necessary, 48 necessary and 22 desirable.

The idea of extensive deployment of towers was not immediately taken up, and not revived until the critical days of 1803. Dundas found Brigadier-General Twiss equally enthusiastic about them. Captain Ford, on Twiss's staff, produced alternative designs for square or circular towers. Like Reynolds' proposals, they were to be sited at close intervals so that they could cross fire with neighbouring towers. The circular form gained acceptance for reasons of cost among military circles but official and political acceptance was another matter. After prolonged delay and obstruction:

> the expensive and diabolical system of tower defence was finally resolved on, to an unprecedented extent and contrary to the opinions of the best and most experienced officers in our service – but it was carried by the influence of the Ordnance people.

The controversy caused delays so that building

56 *Martello towers at Hythe, Kent.*

could not begin until 1805 when the invasion threat was virtually over!

There were seventy-four towers along the south coast from Folkestone to Seaford including the conversion of the keep of Sandgate Castle. Work on them was under the direction of the Board of Ordnance and the Royal Engineers. The main contractor was a William Hobson, who sub-contracted work to local builders. He arranged for a large proportion of the huge quantity of bricks required to be bought up discreetly to avoid stimulating price rises among the London brickmakers, and then to ship them down the Thames.

The south-coast towers were virtually identical (57). Although superficially circular, they were elliptical in plan with the inner and outer wall-faces arranged eccentrically so that the thickest part of the wall faced the most vulnerable seaward side. The towers stand 33ft (10m) high and taper from a thickness of 13ft (4m) at the base on the seaward side to 6ft (1.8m) at the parapet. They were built throughout in brick, bedded in hot lime

mortar (a mixture of lime, ash and hot tallow), which was intended to increase the tower's resistance to bombardment. Entrance to the towers was at first-floor level, by movable ladder if there was no surrounding ditch. If there was a ditch, access was from a drawbridge. The first floor was divided by timber partitions to form living-quarters for the garrison of twenty-four men and one officer. The ground floor was a space for the magazine and stores, with water cisterns below. The flat roof formed the gun platform and was carried on a brick vault supported by a central pier from the base of the tower. The gun platform was reached by a stair in the thickest portion of the wall. Ventilation shafts and chimney flues exited through the parapet. The main armament was a single 24-pounder gun mounted on a traversing carriage pivoting centrally to provide all-round cover. Originally it was intended to mount two carronades of the same calibre as well, all three guns traversing from the same pivot, but this ingenious device does not appear to have been carried out. The garrison was also armed with muskets. These arrangements can be clearly seen at the restored no. 24 at Dymchurch.

57 *Internal arrangements of a south-coast Martello tower.*

The south-coast towers differed from the slightly later East Anglian version which had three guns. They were sited every 500 or 600 yards (457–548m) to give mutual covering fire and some were grouped in pairs either side of the sluices controlling the water-level in Romney Marsh. They were numbered from east to west beginning with no. 1 overlooking East Wear Bay, east of Folkestone. Associated with the south coast towers were the Dymchurch and Eastbourne Redoubts – large circular works with bombproof barrack casemates below the platform for eleven guns above. That at Eastbourne has been renovated and now serves as a military museum (**58**).

While the Martello tower system was being debated, the government accepted Lieutenant Colonel John Brown's plan for a defensive canal from Hythe to the River Rother at Rye to isolate Romney Marsh from the high ground to the rear. A western extension, from the River Brede to Cliff End, cut off Pett Level and Winchelsea Beach.

58 *Eastbourne Redoubt built 1804–10. Model of the redoubt on display in the site museum.*

The civil engineer John Rennie was in charge and much of the canal was completed in the summer of 1805. The canal was not finished, however, until 1809. It was specified to be 62ft (19m) wide at water-level and 9ft (2.7m) deep from the general level of the Marsh. A military road ran along the northern side. There were three military advantages in such a project. It formed a physical defensible barrier, it avoided the need to flood the marshland, and barges on it would provide transport for the deployment of troops.

The Martello towers and the Royal Military Canal were also associated with the field army which was held in an entrenched camp on the Western Heights, Dover, ready to move against a French landing wherever it occurred in the south-east. Much further to the rear was the 'Chalk Ridge Communication' running from Guildford to Rochester along the North Downs and designed to link the military camps which were to be established at the gaps in the Downs. There had earlier been plans for a series of parallel defence lines across Kent and Sussex. At either end of these coastal defences were the complex fortresses of Dover and Portsmouth.

Dover and Chatham

In Dundas's view, if the enemy favoured an eastern advance on London but avoided a confrontation with the Dover defences, he might use the new harbour of Ramsgate as a supply base and for landing his siege train. Whatever the approach on London from the south-east coast, the invading army would have to force the Medway, and with it the Chatham Lines, unless it

59 *Map of the nineteenth/twentieth-century defences in the south-east.*

faced a time-consuming march by way of Maidstone. If this was the French course of action Dover and Chatham assumed a vital strategic importance. With a garrison of 4000 men, it was estimated that Dover might hold out for three or four weeks; Chatham was less predictable (**59**).

Dover was given much attention (**60**). Between 1793 and 1815 close on half-a-million pounds were expended on its defences. In 1798 the then Secretary of State for War summed up its importance:

Without Dover Castle the enemy can have no certain communications; and always supposing that on our shore he finds no means to advance his purpose, the bringing up and placing sufficient artillery to reduce it is a work of slow process and would give time to relieve it, whether he remained in east Kent and made

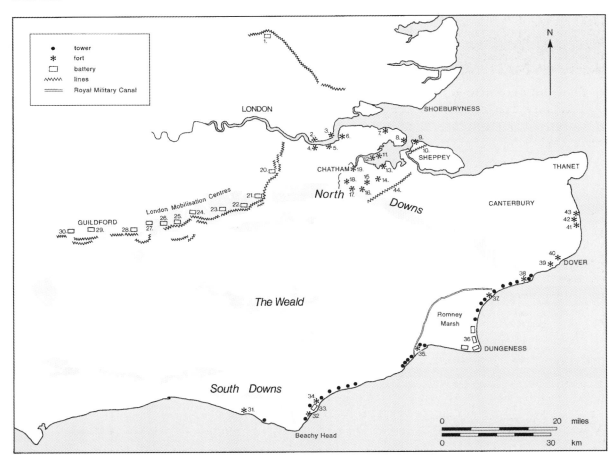

that his chief object or whether he found himself sufficiently strong to press on to the Medway and there wait the result, if in the meantime he could depend on subsisting in the country. The possession to an enemy of Dover Castle, and of the opposite Entrenched Height and of the town and port, fortified in the manner that he would soon accomplish and defended by 6 or 7000 men would establish a sure communication with France and could not be easily wrested from his hands. The conquest of this alone would be to him a sufficient object could he arrive with means of immediately attacking it. Its preservation to us is most important.

The initial impetus was directed at Dover Castle which underwent the most radical changes since the Middle Ages. The Commanding Royal Engineer of the southern district from 1792 to 1809 was Lieutenant-Colonel William Twiss. His first objective at the castle was to strengthen the eastern defences. This involved reducing the height of the medieval outer curtain-wall, backing it with a massive earth rampart, widening and deepening the ditch, and constructing four powerful outworks beyond the counterscarp bank. East

60 *Map of the nineteenth-century defences of Dover in and around the castle, on Western Heights and about the harbour.*

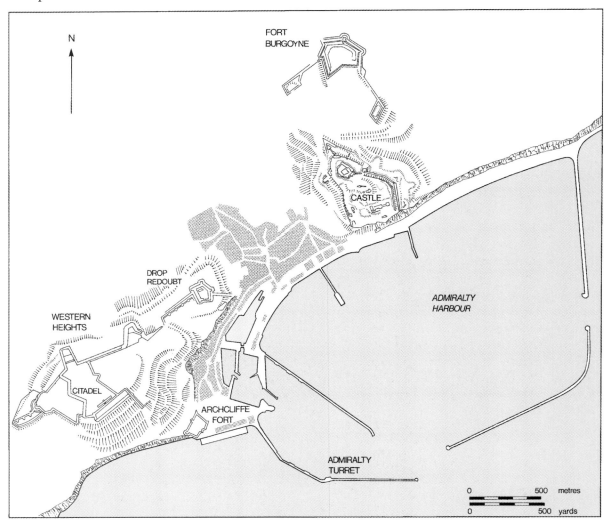

of Avranches Tower was Horseshoe Bastion, next was Hudson's Bastion and on the cliff edge was the East Demi-Baston. Further down the slope from the last two works was the detached East Arrow Bastion. Although described as bastions, these bore no resemblance in plan or function to the conventional angle bastions of the seventeenth and eighteenth centuries. They were enclosed, rectangular, independent earthworks in advance of the main line of the castle defences giving command to the slopes below, thereby allowing the heavy guns on the new rampart to cover the far side of the valley and beyond. Close defence was provided by what were essentially infantry redoubts. The outworks were connected to the castle by underground passages which themselves were protected internally by drawbridges and musketry loops. The western side of the castle, nearest the town, was given better communications in that direction with a new entrance at Canon's Gate wide enough for a column of troops and artillery. The gateway passed below a bombproof vault,

61 *Dover Castle: caponiers in the ditch behind the Spur and in front of St John's Tower.*

one of a line of five casemates. Below the drawbridge was a caponier across the ditch. There was another caponier at the medieval entrance of Constable's Gate. The weak northern side of the castle, which had always caused the defenders trouble, was given 'a sort of Redan', according to Twiss, on the medieval Spur, in an attempt to command the higher ground beyond. Covering the approaches to the redan were the most elaborate local defences imaginable (**61**). Not only was the ditch covered by caponiers, but anyone who managed to get into the underground system could be trapped behind drop-doors or doors operated by remote control, and all the while be under fire from internal musketry positions. The mutilation of the medieval castle was completed by the insertion of massive brick vaults within the keep to provide a bombproof magazine and gun positions on the roof.

Comparatively small sums were spent on the initial fieldworks on the Western Heights between 1793 and 1803. Then, with invasion seemingly imminent, General Sir David Dundas and Colonel Twiss spent two days examining the Heights. Twiss felt that they could be held by 'detached Redoubts with small garrisons'. He had appreciated that the fieldworks could be improved:

> to form this position into an entrenched camp where a corps of five or six thousand men might remain in security and with tolerable convenience and in readiness to move against an enemy wherever required.

The engineer on the spot, Captain William Ford, saw the answer requiring three major detached works. The eastern end of the Downs was given over to the polygonal Drop Redoubt (**62**). At the western end, and the key to the position, was the Citadel. Between the two was the square-fronted, North Centre Bastion. These separate works were connected by the re-formed earlier lines. Despite the colossal sums expended on developing the system of fortifications with their underground works and massive barracks, they remained unfinished at the end of the war. They were not completed until another Napoleon caused a new invasion scare in 1859. Even then, the improved defences did not fulfil Ford's ambition of linking the Western Heights with the castle by means of an earthwork which would close the town of Dover to the north. It was not until 1940 that this objective was achieved by the digging of an anti-tank ditch.

Associated with the works on Western Heights was the refurbishment of Archcliffe Fort above the harbour, which now served as a flank position for

62 *Drop Redoubt, Western Heights, Dover, with its ditch flanked from caponiers at the angles.*

63 Fort Clarence, Rochester. Begun in 1808 and completed 1812; part of the additional defences west of the Chatham Lines to block the crossing of the Medway.

the Drop Redoubt. There was also a requirement for rapid communications between the barracks and defences on the Heights with the town and harbour below. This was solved most ingeniously by Twiss who built the Grand Shaft to connect the two. This remarkable triple staircase winding round a central light-well, enabled a large body of troops to move simultaneously. The barracks have gone but the Grand Shaft remains.

Other entrenched camps and defensive lines were prepared in the Eastern District in the neighbourhood of Chelmsford and Colchester. Since London was reckoned to be the principal objective, a defence line was planned which ran from the River Lea, through Highgate and Hampstead to Holland House and down to the Thames at Chelsea. On the south bank, field-works were thrown up on Shooter's Hill and Blackheath to serve as outworks to the main line of defence. This ran from Deptford through Sydenham and the Norwood Hills and back to the Thames at Wandsworth. To improve communications a floating bridge was constructed between Blackwall Stairs and Greenwich Marshes almost exactly on the line of the present Blackwall Tunnel.

The main land approach to London from the south-east was along the Roman road from Dover and Canterbury (now the A2). Across its path is the River Medway with the main bridge-crossing at Rochester. Associated with the counter-invasion strategy was the creation of a barrier fortress on this most likely line of advance (see **59**).

The earlier defences at Chatham were primarily intended to protect the dockyard, and were continuous lines from the cliff edge above Chatham town across the Brompton heights to the river near the old Gillingham Fort. The new emergency caused the defences to be realigned completely with detached works ringing Rochester. They also guarded the flank of the Chatham Lines, but they provided greater protection for the river-crossing and blocked the approaches from the south and east.

The principal work was Fort Pitt on a spur overlooking the river and with good command to the south. Work was begun in 1805, though the fort was not completed until 1819. Only a partial outline of the fort can now be seen, its significant features long demolished. The next defensive work to be built south of Rochester was Fort Clarence, begun in 1808 and not completed until 1812. This amounted to a substantial road-block controlling the access from the Maidstone road to the Medway by means of a large, three-storey, brick tower (**63**). It resembles nothing so much as a late medieval tower house, complete with round turrets and machicolations. Its main function was to flank a long, brick-revetted ditch with guns firing from casemates in its basement. The height of the tower must have been more for observation than as a lofty gun position. At either end of the ditch were smaller works. Also controlling the north–south roads between Fort Clarence and Fort Pitt were two towers or defensible two-storey brick guardhouses.

Channel Islands

The prospect of invasion was not confined to mainland Britain. The Channel Islands were especially vulnerable and actually suffered attack (see **colour plate 2**). The Tudor monarchs had spent considerably in fortifying Castle Cornet at St Peter Port, Guernsey and Mont Orgueil Castle and later building Elizabeth Castle, both on Jersey.

The use of gun towers for beach defence was pioneered in the Channel Islands in 1779 anticipating by fifteen years the naval action off Cape Mortella, Corsica. Gun towers were nothing new and had been employed occasionally during the seventeenth century at Cromwell's Castle on Tresco, Isles of Scilly and at Mount Batten at Plymouth (see **27**). The initiative for beach defence now came from General Conway, Governor of Jersey, who in a report of May 1778:

> proposed the erection of 30 Round Towers for the defence of the island. Towers to be of masonry, 30–40 feet high and about 500 yards from each other – to be absolutely solid for 10–12 feet from the bottom. Wall above to be strong, pierced with loopholes for musketry in two stages and on the top, where it is proposed to place cannon, a parapet of brick.

The towers took some time to build. Captain Mulcaster appears to have completed four during 1779, but in a letter to General Conway of 1794 only 22 of the intended 32 had been built. Some of the towers, which were intended for 'all the most accessible parts of the coast' were associated with batteries. They were circular; Seymour Tower is the exception from the rest in being square in plan. The towers on Guernsey were slightly different from those on Jersey. They were loopholed for musketry, capable of housing twenty men and mounting a 6-pounder gun on top and were also built at the likely landing places.

In 1782 a new fort, Fort George, was begun above St Peter Port, Guernsey, and remained under construction until 1812. The nucleus of the defensive complex was a regular bastioned fort casemated throughout with barrack accommodation for 13 officers and 250 men. It served as a 'keep of last resort' for a complex of batteries and other works which developed during the early years of the nineteenth century and which replaced Castle Cornet as the main protection for the harbour of St Peter Port and its approaches.

Jersey too lacked a modern citadel to replace Elizabeth Castle. Useful though that was for protecting the approach to the harbour it was unable to provide a focus for the forces on the island and act as a defensible barracks because it was inaccessible at certain times of the tide. Fieldworks on the North and South Hills above St Helier were replaced in 1806 by a large permanent work, Fort Regent, designed and supervised by Lieutenant Colonel John Humphrey. Its situation caused the fort to be of irregular plan, partly protected by natural cliffs.

Elsewhere in Jersey, batteries were maintained, improved and some new towers built. In a letter of January 1811, General Don, the officer in command during the Napoleonic scares, remarked on a new tower on l'Icho Rock. The Tour de Vinde at Noirmont was also begun at the same time. Portelet Bay Tower may have been completed in 1808 and was then ready for its garrison of one sergeant and twelve men. The Rozel Barracks were built in 1810 and a loopholed enclosure wall survives. Military roads were also a feature on the Channel Islands as a means of moving reinforcements quickly to the scene of a landing.

Major-General Sir John Doyle, Lieutenant-Governor of Guernsey, likewise improved the coastal defensive positions. The old castle ruins at Rocquaine were pulled down, the summit of the rock levelled and a very powerful battery erected capable of containing twelve or fourteen guns, semicircular in plan with a substantial masonry front. It was intended that the gorge should be enclosed with casemated accommodation for the garrison. The battery became known as Fort Grey, after the contractor who built it. Elsewhere much attention was given to improving detail, such as the provision of breastworks and thickening of parapets. By 1815 it is estimated that there were 16 forts and barracks and 58 coastal batteries on the island.

Commercial ports

For the British Isles in the latter half of the nineteenth century the risk of full scale invasion was remote. More feasible was the threat of destructive raids by enemy warships on those ports which were of commercial importance and away from the heavily fortified naval bases. Many harbours already had small gun batteries for their protection, which were often erected out of local initiative by the merchants with most to lose. These ports and harbours were armed and often manned by Volunteers during the Napoleonic wars. As the nineteenth century advanced, popular fears and military dissatisfaction with the nation's defences seemed to grow in inverse proportion to the likelihood of an invasion whether from France or from Germany during the early years of the twentieth century. The Royal Commission Report of 1860 had touched on the need to protect the commercial harbours and the issue became more imperative as the century advanced. In 1882 the Morley Committee was appointed by Parliament to inquire into the defences of the mercantile ports.

This committee and subsequent discussions chiefly emphasized the weakness of the east-coast ports. The commercial ports of the south coast, such as Southampton, Dover and Weymouth, already benefited from the protection arising from neighbouring naval establishments or military bases. Precautions had been taken in the 1850s at Littlehampton where a small fort was completed in 1854, continuing a tradition of defensive measures which had begun a century before. Shoreham Redoubt of 1857 was to the same design as Littlehampton. At both there was a degree of experimentation with the introduction of a 'Carnot Wall' in the ditch at the foot of the rampart scarp giving protection for musketry in the *chemin des rondes* behind. This was in addition to the flanking cover to the shallow ditch provided by caponiers. In the West Country there were new batteries built at Dartmouth and St Ives of a simpler kind (see **19**).

The major exception was Newhaven. The combination of a direct railway line with London and a cross-Channel steamer service led to its development as a port. During the 1860s, when the naval bases were being improved, defences at Newhaven were thought essential. Construction on the fort began in 1864 and continued into the 1870s to the design of Lieutenant J.C. Ardagh. It incorporated earlier smooth-bore batteries, and through being built during a time when artillery was in a rapid state of development, its design was adapted to accommodate the most advanced heavier guns and their emplacements. Newhaven has many of the features of a Royal Commission land-fort but is clearly built to higher specifications. There is a quality of craftsmanship and detailing which mark it out. Its unusually wide ditch of 50ft (15m) was flanked by counterscarp galleries with embrasures both for cannon and musketry. The foot of the cliffs on which it stood was covered by a substantially built single-storey brick caponier, linked to the fort above by a tunnel and stairs. The fort was completed at the moment Moncrieff's disappearing carriage and mounting were being adopted. Two 9-inch Moncrieff disappearing guns were placed in deep pits on the eastern rampart overlooking the town and harbour entrance but these have been substantially removed. Most of the ordnance at this time consisted of 9-inch or 10-inch rifled muzzle loaders. It is, however, not just Newhaven's design, novel as it was in some respects, that demands attention today, but because it is the first example of the use of mass concrete as a revetment for ditches in a British fort and perhaps anywhere else in the world.

The development of artificial harbours increased during the late nineteenth century. As well as the defended harbours of refuge at Portland and Alderney, the western docks at Dover required their own fortification (see **60**). The foundations for a battery at the end of the Admiralty Pier were completed in 1872. Ten years later a pair of steam-powered, 80-ton, 16-inch (406mm) rifled muzzle-loading guns were mounted in an armoured turret, the only one of its kind in Britain. The Dover Turret is still there on the Admiralty Pier with its 16-inch guns. These are the only guns of their kind to survive.

5
Twentieth-century total war

Twentieth century defences do not have the 'monumentality' of those of earlier periods. They show an amazing variety and diversity but they have less substance than many former fortifications. Their range extends beyond the battery and its associations and the pillbox. Airfields, radar sites, anti-aircraft positions, command and control centres are just some of the more obvious manifestations. Yet their remains are now mostly fragmentary and often incoherent. They have little visual appeal to match their profound historical interest. Many Second World War sites involve ephemeral earthworks and poor-quality concrete; rusting steel and corrugated iron are usual. The fact that these constructions have survived poorly is partly due to the materials used but more often to well-meaning but unthinking policies for demolition and the removal of 'eyesores' by local and national government in recent years. Belatedly, fifty years on, it is becoming recognized that the tangible remains of a crucial moment in our national history are in great danger of disappearing unrecorded and unappreciated for what they represent. The emergency defences of 1940, in particular, were erected in such a hurry that there is not even the volume of documentary evidence for their construction that exists for other periods.

To discover the nature of twentieth-century defence works, the extent and function of the surviving remains have to be pieced together. There are no maps to provide a lead; twentieth-century defence works are not 'antiquities' to be distinguished by Gothic type. Their remains too are probably less conspicuous on the Channel coastline where 'tidying-up' has been more thorough. Basic archaeological methods are the most appropriate means for filling out the story – aerial photographs, field walking and observation – to be backed up where possible by careful recording and sometimes excavation. Frequently along the cliffs and foreshore there are fragments of concrete construction which may indicate some form of defence work or part of the preparations for D-Day. Even an empty, foul-smelling, rectangular concrete building may be the engine-house for an emergency battery and its searchlights, themselves long gone. The partially filled and eroded depressions in the cliff edge may be the traces of First World War trenches. The remains of wartime airfields or at least old hangars now in use as cattle sheds are more evident. Yet these too are artefacts which are still imperfectly understood and recorded.

While evidence for defence works may be found over the whole length of the south coast, they often have to be searched for. There are also areas where remains are concentrated. This is usually where there has been long continuity in fortification: Dover, Portsmouth and Southsea and Falmouth for example. The much ravaged fortifications of Sheerness and Sheppey still provide traces of First World War defences. Hurst Castle and Landguard Fort retain the batteries and operations towers of the second war. Newhaven and Pendennis Castle have been rearmed appropriately as part of their display as

ancient monuments. The most remarkable piece of continuity of all is at Pevensey where the pillboxes of 1940 are built into the ruins of the Roman 'Saxon Shore' fort and the Norman castle which succeeded it, camouflaged to merge into the ruins (**64**).

First World War
The front line for Home Defence in 1914 was still the Grand Fleet, with a secondary coast organization of submarines and destroyer flotillas. The hypothetical invasion force, 70,000 strong, however, remained a possibility even though on Sir Ian Hamilton's own estimation that, together with horses, guns and transport, the invaders would need at least 150 vessels of various sorts.

Throughout the war, British coasts were guarded by an elaborate system of naval patrols and a local naval defence system. From Scapa Flow the Grand Fleet controlled the North Sea and awaited the emergence of the German navy. The trauma of the bombardment of Hartlepool, Scarborough and Whitby in 1915, however, showed that the Royal Navy was not infallible and the risk of coastal raids, and perhaps invasion,

64 *Pevensey Castle: camouflaged World War II strongpoints built into the castle ruins.*

lowered civilian morale and demanded attention from the military planners. Conventional coastal defences had to be enhanced and manned, measures to counter the new danger of air attack developed, sea communications with France maintained, and the ports protected against submarines and gunboats.

The dispatch of the greater part of the regular army overseas was based on the assumption that the navy could prevent an enemy force larger than 70,000 from landing in Great Britain. Two divisions were held back until the Territorial Force was considered fit to replace them as an adequate protection against enemy raids. Nine territorial divisions and two yeomanry divisions formed a 'Central Force' under the command of Sir Ian Hamilton with a headquarters set up in Tonbridge, Kent. The need to maintain a viable home defence capacity was constantly in Lord Kitchener's mind during the early months of the war and it was a major factor in shaping his policy for the expansion of the army. It meant that

300–500,000 men were kept in Britain despite the demands for manpower on the Western Front. About one-third of these formed the strategic reserve or 'Central Force', while the rest manned the fixed defences and provided local guards. In 1916 there was a review of the strength of the Home Defence Forces. It was now thought that the Germans could reckon on transporting 160,000 men to the east coast between the Wash and Dover and that the navy might not be able to interfere effectively with a landing for twenty-four hours. By 1917 the chances of invasion had lessened. The Admiralty was now willing to lower its figures for a raiding force to 70,000 and the War Office was therefore able to reduce the Home Defence Forces by 40,000.

As well as the long-established batteries and harbour defences of the twenty-six defended ports and naval bases, there were miles of barbed-wire along the south and east coasts, trench systems and pillboxes. None of these measures are good survivors and examples are few. When Field Marshal Sir John French became Commander-in-Chief of all troops in the United Kingdom, greater effort was spent in providing protection for London and the principal ports and naval bases. The Portsdown and Plymouth land-forts were re-equipped. Troops were sent forward to the 'high-water mark' around the coast with the intention of fighting off the Germans before they could establish a bridgehead. The basic strategy was defence in depth relying on fieldworks such as redoubts and trenches. Stop-lines such as the Medway–Swale Line, which included concrete pillboxes, were part of the Thames and Medway Defence Plan which had been worked out before the war (**65**). At Shoeburyness an extensive network of trenches and barbed-wire was constructed with individual blockhouses providing strongpoints. Similar schemes were put in hand around important naval bases such as Portland and Falmouth. On the Isles of Sheppey and Grain hexagonal pillboxes were built in contrast to the circular form favoured in East Anglia.

The coastal batteries had largely been modernized in the years immediately before the outbreak

65 *Medway-Swale World War I stop-line trenches.*

of war. Their armament was rationalized to 9.2-inch, 6-inch and 4.7-inch guns with 6-pounder quick-firing guns to counter fast torpedo boats. Batteries of this kind can be seen in the Falmouth defences (Pendennis and St Mawes Castles and at St Anthony Head) and at Newhaven Fort. Elsewhere, the earlier 12.5-inch and 10-inch rifled muzzle loaders remained in use at Hurst Castle. Here, searchlights were in position in semicircular turrets. During the war barbed-wire entanglements were spread across the beach and around the castle. Machine-guns were mounted on the roof of the west wing. The new coastal batteries, however, were on the east coast such as the sea-forts constructed in the Humber and the Tyne turrets.

A surviving example on Sheppey is Fletcher Battery, now on the fringe of a holiday caravan park (**66**). This was originally built for two 9.2-inch guns with the usual observation posts and magazines. The battery lay within a lozenge-shaped ditched enclosure with salient angles to front and rear and flanked from triple, interlocking, circular pillboxes at either side to create a small fortress. Langdon Battery east of Dover was also enclosed with an unclimbable fence and defended by pillboxes but this now has an architecturally acclaimed coastguard station on top of it. Elsewhere on Sheppey, at Sheerness, there are still the 4.7-inch gun towers of Centre Bastion standing incongruously beside Garrison Point Fort (see **44**).

Complementing such traditional forms of home defence were 16 squadrons of fighter aircraft, 480 anti-aircraft guns and 706 searchlights. The Cabinet, as early as 1908, had appointed a committee under Lord Esher to consider how far Great Britain might be exposed to air bombardment. Air defence appeared for the first time and the Admiralty decided to protect its bases against this new form of attack. Anti-aircraft guns for the first time were installed at naval bases such as Chatham. One of the earliest sites for an anti-aircraft gun is at the Old Needles Battery, Isle of Wight (see **42**). In fact zeppelins did not bomb British targets until January 1915, to widespread alarm. In 1917 the twin-engined *Gotha* came into service and the first daylight raids on the south-eastern counties and London occurred in May of that year.

Airfields proliferated along the south-east coast. Many of them, whose names were to be again familiar in the Second World War, had their origins in the First. Ford opened as a Royal Flying Corps establishment in 1918. Tangmere was another. Each airfield comprised six or seven hangars for the aircraft, workshops, magazines, firing ranges, 'bomb dropping towers' and 'buzzing and picture target' huts, as well as barracks. It is mainly early hangars which survive today. One of the most accessible of the early airbases is Calshot. It was opened by the Royal Naval Air Service in March 1913 and some of its seaplane and flying boat hangars remain (**67**).

The emergence of aerial bombardment stimulated counter-measures which required an early-warning system. Radio interceptions which had been developed by the navy 'Y' stations were turned to picking up zeppelin communications and sound mirrors began to appear on the English north-east coast. Civil defence was, however, limited and early bomb shelters were natural caves such as those at Ramsgate and Chislehurst.

Control of the Straits of Dover was crucial. In 1905 the army established a Fire Command Post at Dover Castle to control and direct the seaward

66 *Fletcher Battery, Sheppey. Battery for two 9.2-inch guns commanding the approaches to the Medway. It was built in 1915 and was surrounded by wire and earthworks flanked by concrete pillboxes.*

67 *Calshot Castle with the remaining flying-boat hangars. The Royal Naval Air Service station opened in 1913 and became responsible for Channel patrols.*

68 *Dover: Admiralty Port War Signal Station built on top of an earlier gun emplacement.*

gun batteries. On the outbreak of war in 1914, the Admiralty transferred its Port War Signal Station here from Western Heights and it remains on the cliff edge of the castle enclosure (**68**). Dover had become a key naval station; the new 610-acre (247ha) Admiralty Harbour giving the only safe haven for warships between the Nore and Portsmouth. Throughout the First World War, Dover provided escorts for the troop and supply convoys to France and mounted patrols in the Dover Straits to counter enemy submarines and surface ships. Over 400 vessels formed the Dover Patrol.

Boom defences against submarines and torpedo boats were adopted at most ports. Elements can still be seen at the mouth of the Medway. One of the more substantial monuments of the First World War, however, is the Nab Tower now set in the approaches to the Solent. It was one of up to six anti-submarine concrete gun towers built at Shoreham, to be towed out to sea to supplement the minefields and steel boom nets between the Goodwin Sands and Dunkirk. The war ended before the towers were finished. The single completed tower was towed out and sunk close to the Nab sandbanks 5 miles (8km) off Bembridge, Isle of Wight, and used as a navigational aid by Trinity House.

'The bomber will always get through'

(Stanley Baldwin, House of Commons, 1932)

In 1922, a 23 squadron (14 bomber and 9 fighter) scheme of air expansion based on the Steel–Bartholomew Plan was announced. It defined an aircraft fighting zone some 15 miles (24km) deep extending round London from Duxford to Salisbury Plain. There was an inner and outer artillery zone for the close defence of London with the deployment of searchlights (**69**). Along the coast there were to be sound detectors with advanced observer posts in front of the aircraft fighting zone. This plan was extended in the following year by the 'Fifty-Two Squadron Scheme' inspired by the disparity between the Royal Air Force and an expanding French airforce.

In 1933 came the first meeting of the Defence Requirements Committee. It took as its point of departure that, for the moment, the chief danger lay in the Far East. Nevertheless it soon reached the conclusion that the 'ultimate potential enemy' was Germany. The committee drew attention to the risk of air attack and the new conception of a 'knock-out blow' from the air. With Germany now seen as the potential enemy, the Reorientation Committee reported early in 1935 in favour of a continuous defence zone from the Tees round London to the Solent. Defended ports such as those of Dover and Portsmouth would have their own defences.

This led to an 'expansion period' for the RAF. Emphasis was placed on the bomber but there was also an air-defence strategy involving early-warning systems, definition of fighter commands, and associated anti-aircraft guns and searchlights.

The tangible result of the 'expansion period' was the construction and reconstruction of many airfields. As well as many distinctive features such as hangars and watch/control towers, a clear architecture for domestic structures such as barracks and the officers' mess emerges. There are two styles: one which dates from the end of the 1920s and the other from the late 1930s. In addition are the operation blocks, armoury, station HQ, guardhouse, engine-testing house, blast shelters, parachute stores, machine-gun butts and air-raid shelters. Some of the 1920s' operations buildings survive at Hawkinge (**70**). The restrained neo-Georgian officers' mess at Biggin Hill is typical of the 'expansion period'.

One of the most interesting structures of this period is the sound mirror which followed pioneering work in early-warning systems during the first war. These can be concrete dishes as at Dover or lengths of wall (200ft/6m long) at Greatstone near Dungeness and Hythe (**71**). Work on acoustic mirrors, however, stopped in 1935 as Radio Direction Finding Stations or Radar, as it came to be known, developed at Bawdsey Manor and Orfordness, Suffolk. The first system was the Chain Home (CH) of about twenty stations from the Tyne to Southampton. The masts were about

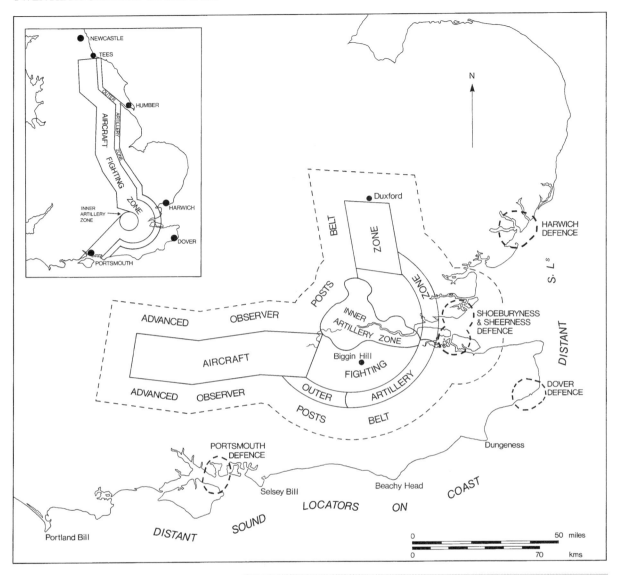

69 *Pattern of air defence in 1923 with a revised scheme (inset) of the 1930s (After B. Collier 1957).*

70 *RAF Hawkinge, Kent: operations block of 1929 with a pillbox on the extreme left.*

71 *Greatstone sound mirrors near Dungeness: a long concrete wall with two bowl mirrors alongside.*

72 *Three surviving Chain Home masts at Swingate, Dover.*

250ft (76m) tall and some can still be seen at Swingate, Dover (72). These were later strengthened by additional Chain Home Low (CHL) stations whose purpose was to detect low-flying aircraft. A residual CH station remains at Dunkirk west of Canterbury. Only one steel transmitter tower is intact but the bases of three others survive as well as those for the wooden receiving towers. The whole complex is partially surrounded by light anti-aircraft positions and pillboxes.

Appreciation of the vulnerability of the civilian population to bombing led to the appointment of an Air Raid Precautions committee as early as 1924, and the first full-time ARP official came in 1933. The bombing of Guernica during the Spanish Civil War in 1937 not only caused revulsion but demonstrated the sort of casualties which might be involved and encouraged fear of a 'knock-out blow' from the air. Preparations were made for public and household (Anderson) air-raid shelters, protection from the threat of poison gas attack and for the evacuation of populations from the most vulnerable areas. The 'Munich crisis' of 1938 was the stimulus for a sudden rehearsal of air-raid precautions.

In naval terms everything depended upon the successful defence of the British Isles and the sea-routes which supplied so much of Britain's food and raw materials. Apart from the Home Fleet, the naval organization consisted of four commands:

Western Approaches (Plymouth); Portsmouth Command: the Nore Command (Chatham); and the Coast of Scotland (Rosyth). Soon after the Treaty of Washington of 1922 had modified the relative naval strengths of the powers, the Admiralty drew up a new list of ports which ought to be protected against bombardment by capital ships; penetration or close approach by submarines, light surface craft, blockships and minelayers; air attack; assaults by landing-parties and bombardment by cross-Channel guns. It included some thirty places in the United Kingdom and the Channel Islands. In the circumstances envisaged, home ports seemed unlikely to be bombarded at long range by armoured ships. Accordingly no guns larger than 9.2-inch were recommended although in 1934 the Defence Requirements Committee observed that the home coast defences were completely out of date'. At the beginning of December 1937 the Air Ministry agreed that the primary role of Coastal Command should be 'trade-protection, reconnaissance and cooperation with the Royal Navy'. By the outbreak of war, the most heavily defended areas were London, Thames/Medway and Portsmouth/Southampton in the south. There was an anti-submarine boom at Portsmouth between the nineteenth-century sea-forts, and a repeat of the mine barrage at Dover at the southern exit from the North Sea. The boom at Shoeburyness is still very visible. The application

73 *Newhaven Fort, coast artillery radar position.*

of radar to coast defence can be seen at Dover Castle, Newhaven Fort (**73**) and East Tilbury.

On land, lessons were learnt from the Spanish Civil War and, once the world war had started, from the early German campaigns in Poland, the Low Countries and France. In particular there was the co-ordinated assault by armoured vehicles and dive-bombers at a speed which gave the word *blitzkrieg* to the English language. Liddell Hart in 1939 had warned of the danger of parachutists and this was borne out by the use of airborne forces to capture the Dutch airfields and to incapacitate the newly built Belgian fort of Eben Emael.

For the British Expeditionary Force's movement to France in 1939, standard designs for concrete pillboxes had been prepared and were available for the coming invasion crisis. According to French calculations six pillboxes were required for each kilometre. General Ironside was very interested in the construction, use and deployment of pillboxes and the use of mechanical diggers for anti-tank obstacles, which were to stand him in good stead when the crisis for Britain came in 1940.

Operation 'Sealion'

On 27 May 1940 General Ironside became Commander-in-Chief Home Forces of Great Britain. He expected a German attack in four stages: indiscriminate and widespread bombing to break down public morale, concentrated air attacks on ports and shipping to cut off supplies, intensive attack on the RAF and supporting industry to gain air supremacy, and invasion both from the sky and sea. The vulnerable area of the coastline was thought to be between the Wash and Folkestone but as the Germans advanced into northern France the 'danger area' was extended to any port on the southern coastline which lay within 200 miles (322km) of a German-occupied airfield (**74**).

At the outbreak of war, Coast Artillery had a total of twenty-one 9.2 inch, forty-one 6 inch and thirty-one 12-pounder guns in the defended ports of Portsmouth (including the Isle of Wight), Plymouth, Falmouth, Portland, Dover, Newhaven, Thames and Medway, which were manned by Territorial regiments. Following the evacuation of the British Expeditionary Force from Dunkirk, it was decided to provide additional emergency coast-defence batteries round the whole of the British Isles whose job it was to protect the minor

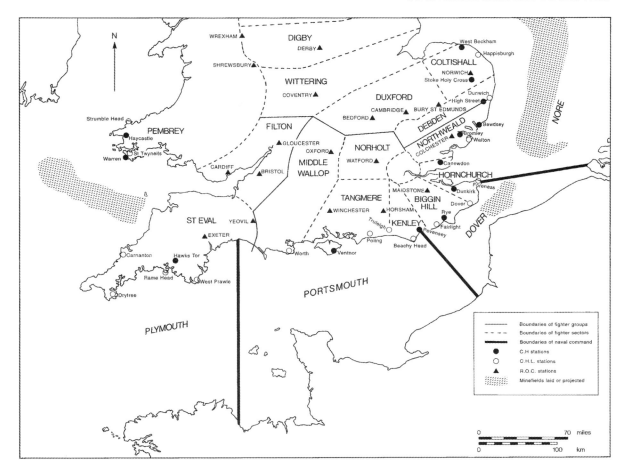

74 *Map of maritime defence, radar chain and fighter sectors, 1940 (After B. Collier 1957).*

ports and cover every vulnerable beach. The guns were those salvaged from obsolete warships scrapped by the Royal Navy after the First World War. Along the Channel coast, thirteen minor ports were protected in addition to the defended ports, and there were, besides forty-five beach batteries.

Eight of Ironside's available fifteen infantry divisions were devoted primarily to coast defence 'with their rear elements disposed to deal with airborne attack'. Three divisions were in a GHQ Reserve on the line Northampton–North London–Aldershot and the 2nd Armoured Division was also in reserve in Lincolnshire. The coast from Sheppey to Rye was manned by the 1st London Division with twenty-three field guns. It had no anti-tank guns, no armoured vehicles, no medium machine-guns and about a sixth of the anti-tank rifles to which it was entitled. This

was a common situation. The Chiefs of Staff admitted that 'should the Germans succeed in establishing a force with its vehicles in this country, our army forces have not got the offensive power to drive it out'.

The inability of the Royal Navy to prevent Germany landing troops in Norway in the teeth of superior allied surface strength was a depressing lesson. Ironside's general plan was to have a defensive 'crust' along the beaches to defeat minor enterprises and to pass back information. Behind were road-blocks and inland stop-lines to prevent armoured penetration, using small fast moving units to deal with parachutists and airborne troops, and a general reserve north and south of London for counter-attacks towards East

Anglia or the south coast. Improvised armoured cars were armed with bren-guns. Ironside defined the duties of the Local Defence Volunteers as undertaking the static defence of their village by road-blocks to prevent an armoured column moving through, collecting information from bicycle patrols issuing from the village, and relying on Molotov cocktails hurled from house windows to deal with tanks. In the meantime he was collecting a mobile reserve.

The pivot of Ironside's plan was a GHQ line of anti-tank obstacles covering London and the Midlands, supported by a series of command, corps and divisional stop-lines sited further forward to delay an advance and giving time for mobile forces to move from the GHQ Reserve, but the stop-lines still lacked anti-tank guns.

It was the idea of static defence which dismayed General Alan Brooke when he was reappointed C.-in-C. Southern Command on 26 June 1940. He disliked the massive concrete road-blocks at the approaches to most towns and

75 *Layout of an 'emergency' battery. The reconstruction drawing shows two 6-inch gun positions with magazine between and the battery observation post behind. To the right is a searchlight position and to the rear pillboxes on the barbed-wire perimeter* (After P. Kent 1988).

many villages. It was a system that he had encountered earlier in France and thought it unsound. Alan Brooke believed that the defence of the country must rest on different principles. A light line of defence would need to be held on the coast to delay landings but the main effort should come from the mobile reserves. He believed that reliance on a static line would require too many troops to man it. To be fair to Ironside, he too would have liked a mobile defensive strategy but had to manage with few resources. By July, circumstances had changed with the return of the British Expeditionary Force and the beginnings of a supply of anti-tank weapons.

General Alan Brooke replaced Ironside on 19 July. The Inter-Service Committee on Invasion anticipated a frontal attack through Kent and Sussex. Indeed, the revised 'Sealion' plan of September 1940 showed landing areas between Brighton and Folkestone. Early in August, Alan Brooke proclaimed his intention of stamping out the idea of linear defence and making mobile-offensive action the keynote of his strategy. Stop-lines were given second place. New construction was to be limited to the formation of 'nodal points' for all-round defence at important road junctions and centres of communication. Anti-tank guns moved forward to cover the beach obstacles and debouchments.

When Germany attacked the Soviet Union in June 1941 the threat of invasion would seem to have been eased. The Commander-in-Chief, however, still saw the danger of a sudden swift descent, unheralded by preliminary air bombardment, by an enemy prepared to take big risks and relying on speed, mass and surprise. He needed sufficient armoured formations to defeat the greatest volume of tanks which the Germans could get ashore. He required 43,000 men for coast defence as well as volunteers for the local defence of airfields and other vulnerable places. His continued strategy was to hold the coast as an outpost line retaining the bulk of his troops in local and GHQ reserves as fully mobile counter-attack formations.

Alan Brooke was himself succeeded by Lieutenant General Sir Bernard Paget in December 1941. Economies in coastal defence began as early as 1942 when fifty batteries not directly guarding ports or harbours were declared redundant. Seventy-one batteries out of the 260 existing in autumn 1943 could be dispensed with. Seventy-five of the 260 were 'Home Guard' batteries.

What can be seen today of the anti-invasion measures? The most substantial artefact was the emergency battery (**75**). Typically this comprised two 6-inch naval guns, with brick and concrete 'gun-houses' over the emplacements for protection against aerial straffing, and two searchlights; though at a number of lesser locations 4.7-inch and 4-inch guns were mounted as well as some other calibres (**76**). Alongside the emplacements

76 *'Mounting a beach defence gun.'*

were a battery observation post, shelters for the gunners, magazine, and an engine-house for the lights. There were variants, often due to other calibres of guns being pressed into service. Accommodation for the garrisons was usually in separate camps nearby. Local defence could include pillboxes, light anti-aircraft guns and guardrooms.

A good example of a 6-inch coast battery still retaining its gun-house is the Half Moon Battery at Pendennis Castle, Falmouth, together with its restored battery observation post in the Elizabethan rampart above (see **colour plate 8**). On the shore close by are the bases for the searchlights serving the now demolished twin-6-pounder battery of Middle Point (see **31**). St Martin's Battery on Dover's Western Heights no longer has any armament but Newhaven Fort has a 6-inch gun on its correct mounting (**77**) and cover over the other 6-inch emplacement. Twin-6-pounder positions remain at Landguard Fort opposite Harwich (**78**).

Of the coastal crust, besides the beach batteries, there were tank obstacles, trenches and pillboxes (**79**). Beaches were mined and obstructed and roads leading inland blocked. Builders' scaffolding armed with mines was erected below high-water mark for about 70 miles (112km) of coastline. About 300 miles (483km) of scaffolding, besides buried mines, were used as beach obstructions. Anti-tank ditches were dug

77 *Newhaven Fort, 6-inch gun with magazine below.*

and obstacles erected, generally blocks, cylinders and 'dragon's teeth' or 'pimples'.

These have all been vulnerable to coastal erosion, sea defence and deliberate destruction and removal. There are few good concentrations remaining along the south coast and only occasional examples of particular types can now be seen. At Eastney and Milford, Hampshire, are examples of anti-tank blocks. Generally these would have been associated with pillboxes, often

78 *Landguard Fort: twin-6-pounder position at Darrell's Battery with directing tower behind.*

hexagonal, on the beaches or just inland. Less obvious today are the associated trench systems and dug-outs. Occasionally there are lengths of anti-tank wall as at Norman's Bay, Sussex. An unusual grouping of pillboxes and strongpoints is at Porthcurno, Cornwall, as defence against raids on the terminus of the international submarine cable. Here are clifftop pillboxes and close beach defence from infantry positions and weapon pits. The camouflaged strongpoints at Pevensey Castle have already been mentioned (see **64**). Another example of continuity are the anti-tank defences – pillbox behind the medieval curtain-wall, blocks and concrete parapet – at Dover Castle, commanding the approaches to Constable's Gate (**80**). There is also the anti-tank position built into the foot of Horseshoe Bastion.

Inland, back from the beaches, were road-blocks that can still be seen at some roadsides. The Petroleum Warfare Department, created early in June 1940, produced schemes for flame-fougasses along roads. Forty-gallon (182 litre) drums with inflammable materials were installed in lieu of minefields, particularly on the long hill between Dover and Canterbury.

Behind the coastline there was a determined effort to prevent the sort of rapid armoured

79 Hayling Island: pillbox on the sea-wall.

advance which had characterized the German offensives in Poland, the Low Countries and France. Stop-lines were based on natural obstacles such as rivers or canals and railway lines or contrived by the digging of anti-tank ditches across the gaps. The principal line was the GHQ Line extending from Bristol to Maidstone in the south and in the east from Maidstone to Cambridge and the Wash, thence to Richmond in Yorkshire (see **9**). In places there were lines of anti-tank pillboxes co-ordinated to give interlocking arcs of 2-pounder anti-tank gunfire. Elsewhere, Corps and Divisional lines were constructed between the GHQ Line and the coast, often extending north–south such as the Taunton stop-line and those in Kent and Sussex. The construction of one of these works from Newhaven to Eridge has been described by the civil engineer responsible. Among these works were defensive strongpoints of anti-tank ditches and pillboxes, known as 'hedgehogs', notably at Blandford in Dorset.

Pillboxes are now the most visible survival of these lines. There were about ten official types, of which the best known is the ubiquitous hexagonal Type 22, suitable for about five light automatic weapons, and Type 24, an irregular hexagon. There are, besides, others which are hexagonal or pentagonal, rectangular or circular. Many do not conform to any standard type and may have a restricted regional distribution. While most are for rifles and light machine-guns, others (Type 28 and 28A) were designed for 2-pounder anti-tank guns. Some have an enclosed open area with a central pillar for mounting an anti-aircraft light machine-gun. At first the reinforced concrete walls were commonly 18in (46cm) thick but later versions

80 Dover Castle: anti-tank gun embrasure between the two towers and anti-tank dragon's teeth on the earth rampart in the foreground.

and designs had 3ft (90cm) thick walls. A good sequence of coastal pillboxes relating to a railway line is at Christchurch, Dorset. To these must be added strongpoints, often a machine-gun position contrived within an existing structure, or just a loopholed wall commanding a road junction.

Anti-glider precautions were common whether in the form of ditches or obstacles across open land. They are now hard to find. Perhaps the best examples are those at Sutton Hoo, Suffolk, preserved amid the Anglo-Saxon barrow cemetery.

Another unusual construction is the resistance cell for Home Guard Auxiliary Units. These were small underground operations posts for resistance fighters following invasion. The artefact, however, most commonly associated with the Home Guard is the concrete cylinder with a brass mounting on the top for a spigot mortar or Blacker Bombard, another anti-tank weapon.

Battle of Britain

At the end of May 1940, Air Chief Marshal Dowding expressed the view that 'the continued existence of the nation, and all its services, depends upon the Royal Navy and the Fighter Command'. The resulting 'Battle of Britain' lies outside the scope of this book but the airfields from which it was fought are archaeologically relevant.

Along the southern and south-eastern coasts and their hinterland were some 110 military airfields of various types and dates. Most were fighter bases or those associated with the Fleet Air Arm. The bomber bases tended to be further inland and in the Midlands and East Anglia. Fighter airfields associated with the Battle of Britain such as Biggin Hill, Hawkinge, Manston, Detling, Tangmere, North Weald and others owed their existence to the 'expansion period' if not earlier. Most have some physical remains from 1940, though bomb damage, as at Tangmere, accounted for the loss of most of its pre-war buildings, and no airfield has survived to anything approaching its wartime integrity. Perhaps the grass field of Hawkinge might have had that potential but airfields are tempting areas for commercial exploitation.

There is no 'standard layout' for an airfield, yet all have similarities. Some have permanent runways, others retained the original grassed surfaces, some have Technical and Domestic sites which are either grouped together or are on opposite sides of the camp access. Those wartime airfields which did not originate in the 'expansion period' or earlier tend to be the least well preserved because they were created in an emergency with temporary buildings unlikely to survive unless the airfield continued in active use after the war. Those of the 'expansion period' are much more solid even if they are architecturally predictable. In addition to these main airfields, there were also dispersal airfields, relief landing grounds and decoys.

Airfield buildings involve many varieties of hangar, and because these are likely to offer alternative uses one can expect to find this type of survival. Watch offices are also familiar and may have renewed life if the airfield has retained commercial use, as at Shoreham. Also at Shoreham is one of the more unusual airfield structures: a dome trainer.

The possibility of airborne attack was a significant worry. The Air Staff calculated that fewer than 5000 parachutists could temporarily paralyse the country's air defences by attacking seven vital aerodromes in south-east England, which might then pave the way for bomber raids and landings from troop carriers. In theory, Air Ministry policy before 1943 was for all stations, including relief landing grounds and satellites, within 20 miles (32km) of selected ports to be considered Class 1. They were to be provided with pillboxes around the perimeter, all designed to overlook the airfield. A second series of pillboxes was sited to cover the approaches and dispersal points. Rifle pits were sited around the hangars and station buildings. Sometimes these pits were developed into elaborate Seagull Trenches of flattened W-shaped plan. Class 2 airfields, not strategically placed but responsible for repelling seaborne attacks, had a 25 per cent reduction in pillboxes for inward defence. For Class 3, a single ring of pillboxes with all-round fire capability was considered sufficient.

81 *RAF Hawkinge airfield: Pickett-Hamilton pillbox.*

In practice, local-defence decisions were taken pragmatically by commanders and no standards emerged. There was usually an observation post or strongpoint with all-round visibility which served as a Battle HQ. Additionally, there were specialist defences avoiding interference with the manoeuvring of planes, such as the Pickett-Hamilton Retractable Fort (**81**), usually arranged in groups of three, the Alan Williams Turrets and the 'mushroom' pillbox. The RAF often produced its own designs of pillbox with anti-aircraft gun pits attached.

Apart from the fighter plane, the other form of defence against air attack was the anti-aircraft gun battery together with searchlights. The 3-inch gun adopted between the wars was superseded by heavy anti-aircraft defences based on three types of gun: 3.7-inch, 4.5-inch and the 5.25-inch, the latter introduced in 1943. All these required extensive concrete installations, with protective pits for the guns, a command centre with communications rooms and platforms for predictors, range and height finders, magazines, shelters and local defences (**82**). Each 'gun defended area' had a Gun Operations Room connected directly with Fighter Group operations. The heavy anti-aircraft guns were generally grouped in clusters of four, six or eight

82 *Richmond Park anti-aircraft battery.*

83 *Aerial view of Maker Heights anti-aircraft battery.*

84 *Maunsell Army fort off the Thames Estuary.*

with associated buildings. The 3.7-inch and 4.5-inch guns were mounted in octagonal emplacements with blast walls of concrete about 5ft (1.5m) high with built-in crew shelters and ammunition lockers protected by steel doors. The 5.25-inch guns were in deep circular pits which contained the pedestal and there were adjacent underground magazines. Anti-aircraft gun sites are now uncommon but good examples are at East Tilbury, Hayling Island and Maker Heights west of Plymouth (**83**).

As well as being mobile, the 40mm Bofors guns could have fixed positions such as those on the eastern rampart of Dover Castle, or be mounted on special concrete towers as at Dunkirk radar station near Canterbury and Crawley in Sussex. All anti-aircraft defences could assume a secondary ground defence role. In addition to the light anti-aircraft guns were the 'Z' rocket batteries

frequently manned by the Home Guard. The equipment of a searchlight site consisted of a 90cm projector with, in most cases, a sound locator. Each searchlight site was equipped with a light machine-gun for use against low-flying aircraft and for ground defence.

In 1943 to counter minelaying aircraft and to close a gap in the London air defences, a number of isolated sea-forts were built off the Thames and Medway estuaries and the east coast. These Maunsell forts were each capable of mounting four 3.7-inch guns, two 40-millimetre guns, a searchlight and a radar set. There were two types (Navy and Army), the former were not unlike the Nab Tower, the latter were groups of platforms on legs linked by horizontal catwalks (**84**).

A method of distracting enemy bombers was the use of decoys which were in use from June 1940. Each airfield had a decoy site. It is said that these were bombed twice as many times as genuine airfields between June and October that year. There were sixty decoy Starfish sites diverting attention from real docks or armament factories. In April 1941 one particular raid on Portsmouth resulted in decoy sites receiving 90 per cent of bombs dropped.

Air-raid shelters were the principal structures associated with Civil Defence. Before the war there was a degree of preparation against the anticipated bombs. It varied from the outdoor surface shelter in public places, such as lined and covered trenches in the royal parks, to open-topped brick street shelters and the individual Anderson shelters to be dug into back gardens. By 1940, communal shelters to an improved design were erected in streets and playgrounds. Shelter from bombing was also taken in natural caves or in man-made tunnels, such as the deep underground railway tunnels in London or in the cliffs at Dover. Air-raid shelters are now mainly to be found in the vicinity of military camps and barracks as at Dover Castle and Shorncliffe. Structures such as decontamination centres, fire-watch shelters, static water tanks to hold 5000 gallons (22,730 litres) and other Emergency Water Supply (EWS) tanks are now hardly to be found.

Bombardment and counter bombardment

From May 1940, naval command of the Dover Straits was lost. The destroyers based at Dover were withdrawn to Portsmouth and overall control was fought out in the sky. Dover itself had but four 6-inch and two 9.2-inch guns to protect the harbour. Vice-Admiral Ramsay now suggested that a number of long-range guns should be installed in the Dover area to match the German batteries in the Pas de Calais. A special kind of cross-Channel bombardment and counter-bombardment was begun. Fixed batteries for 14-inch guns were constructed with emplacements for guns, two nicknamed 'Winnie' and 'Pooh' (**85**). There were also railway guns and dummy batteries. Only scraps of evidence remain of the Dover counter-bombardment batteries at Wanstone and South Foreland apart from the underground plotting room the battery plotting room, and magazines.

Elsewhere along the Channel, destruction was already being caused by German submarines and minefields. An early menace to shipping was the German magnetic mine. Its effects were countered by altering a ship's magnetic field. Degaussing establishments in dockyards and elswhere have left their own specialist structures.

The hazards of mine and torpedo were amplified by the activity of fast German E-boats operating from French harbours. Boom defences were provided in the Thames at Canvey Island and Shoeburyness, in the Solent and Plymouth and some of these have left their traces, notably at Shoeburyness. There were a number of light booms put in place outside anchorages such as Falmouth (see **colour plate 5**). These obstacles were associated with quick-firer batteries and searchlights such as those in the breakwaters of Dover and Portland Harbours, and by new twin-6-pounder batteries and associated searchlights at places like Falmouth (see **31**). These harbour defences, however, were easy casualties of peacetime with only ghosts of their former existence or surviving examples at monuments like Hurst Castle.

Other manifestations of coastal naval warfare were defensive torpedo stations and inshore

85 *'Pooh' at St Margaret's Bay, Dover, one of two 14-inch counter-bombardment guns.*

controlled minefields. The latter were operated from two- or three-storey reinforced concrete observation and control towers (XDOs). Good examples of XDO stations are at Coalhouse Fort, East Tilbury (**86**) and at Eastney.

Command and control

The Commander-in-Chief Home Forces set up an Advanced Headquarters close to the Cabinet War Room in Whitehall. Should Germans have landed, the War Cabinet, Chiefs of Staff and the Naval, General and Air Staffs were to stay in London, but if driven from Whitehall they would move to duplicate War Rooms in the suburbs. The Whitehall War Rooms are now displayed to the public by the Imperial War Museum and

provide an insight into the trappings of command at the highest level. There were other deep-cellared 'fortresses' elsewhere in central London and the Admiralty Citadel complete with machine-gun loops stands at the corner of Horse Guards Parade. Elsewhere command and control centres were more distinctly underground.

In August 1939 Vice-Admiral Ramsay was responsible for denying the Dover Straits to enemy naval forces and for the safety of allied cross-Channel shipping. He saw the potential of the casemate tunnels, dug in 1797 into the cliff below Dover Castle, as a bombproof naval headquarters below the Port War Signal Station of the First World War. Ramsay and his staff principally occupied the easternmost casemate. For nine days in late May and early June 1940 these tunnels were to be the nerve-centre controlling the naval part of the evacuation of 338,000 troops from the

beaches of Dunkirk. In the words of David Divine, who himself had manned one of the 'little ships':

> It is given to few men to command a miracle. It was so given to Bertram Home Ramsay, and the frail iron balcony that juts from the embrasure of the old casemate in the Dover cliff was the quarterdeck from which he commanded one of the great campaigns in the sea story of Britain.

With the danger of invasion now present, the Dover Castle tunnels took on even greater importance and by 1943 they had become a Combined Headquarters for all three services. Throughout the war there was constant action in the Channel whether from the air or between German E-boats and Royal Naval craft and from long-range

86 *Coalhouse Fort XDO position for controlling a defence minefield.*

bombardment. Convoys and individual merchant ships continually sought to pass through. The gun batteries between the North Foreland and Hastings were controlled from here, as were naval ships. There was close communication with the RAF and intelligence gathering and plots from the radar chain whose masts were a prominent feature on the clifftop east of the castle.

With growing pressure for space in the existing tunnels the system was extended in 1941. An upper level of tunnels named 'Annexe' was excavated a little to the west of the Napoleonic level known as 'Casemate Level'. Another tunnel was dug west of the three eastern tunnels of 'Casemate Level'. This was for the General Post Office which had charge of all the land communications. It was

111

87 *Duxford: reconstructed fighter-control operations room.*

here that the main telephone exchange was located. The new complex for the Combined Headquarters was, in turn, part of the long-term preparations for the invasion of France and available as a duplicate headquarters in case the main operations centre behind Portsmouth at Southwick was put out of action (**colour plate 12**).

In 1942 another system of tunnels 50ft (15m) below the level of the Napoleonic tunnels was completed and codenamed 'Dumpy'. After the navy had abandoned the tunnels in 1958, these were adapted to form one of ten regional seats of government and were intended to function during and after a nuclear attack. New communications equipment, air-filtration plant and improved generators were installed. On the Casemate Level, the three eastern tunnels, once Ramsay's headquarters, the local command centres for the coastal artillery, the anti-aircraft operations room and the old telephone exchange, were abandoned. The western group of tunnels were modernized to become dormitories and mess rooms. The largest of the six military telephone exchanges and a repeater station have been re-created in the Combined Services casemates.

To understand how the control of the defending fighter squadrons was achieved and the advantages provided by radar for both air and coastal defence, a visit to the reconstructed operations rooms at places such as Duxford is necessary (**87**). The site evidence is now very sparse.

Similar to the fighter-control operations rooms were those of the Royal Observer Corps. One of these survives in the suburbs of Winchester and was set out as a museum but its future is in doubt. ROC posts themselves were often flimsy affairs but a few more substantial than the rest can be seen. An exhibition at Newhaven Fort demonstrates their activities. On a smaller scale there are a number of substantial Port War Signal Stations, besides that already mentioned at Dover Castle, at all the major and many minor naval ports for the control of shipping. These can be identified at many ports.

Civil Defence control centres were another feature of the war. They were often in existing houses or office buildings and as such have subsequently remained in some form of public use and occupation even if their internal details and equipment may be missing. Some retained a defence function by becoming regional seats of government of a nuclear age.

Epilogue

Most emergency batteries were put into a state of care and maintenance well before the end of the Second World War. The atomic bomb and the ballistic missile then revolutionized warfare and changed irrevocably earlier forms of national defence. Although Sweden and Norway have highly developed coastal artillery systems to the present day, Britain abolished coast defence in 1956. The forts, batteries and many other military works in the hands of the Ministry of Defence have been made redundant and efforts continue to be made to dispose of them.

National defence has since rested on the concept of the nuclear deterrent and its manifestations have been certain military airfields and naval bases, the early-warning systems, Royal Observer Corps centres and regional seats of government. Even these are becoming redundant and far-sighted individuals are considering which examples should be preserved for future generations as part of the archaeological heritage.

The contribution that fortifications have made to the development of the historic landscape is therefore considerable. Their recognition and understanding has greatly increased in recent years through the fieldwork and publications of such organizations as the Fortress Study Group and by many groups of enthusiasts who have carried out investigation and research on a local level or who have set about restoring a previously abandoned fort. It is a subject which interests a growing number of people, and not before time, since the archaeological evidence is much at risk from ignorance and neglect.

Over the past 500 years expenditure on and construction of defence works have been repeatedly questioned and at times treated with obloquy. Members of Parliament have railed against the costs and usurpation of private property, members of golf clubs have protested at the siting of an anti-aircraft battery on their course. Yet at times of emergency, whether in 1539 or 1940, all sections of the population, regardless of age and sex, have joined in the common activity of digging trenches and watching the coasts and skies. Defence of home and community is an enduring human purpose and it has left its mark on the British landscape.

Glossary

advanced works Additional works beyond the glacis but still commanded from the main defences.

barbette Breastwork of a battery sufficiently low so that guns may fire over it without the need for embrasures.

barbican Outwork for the protection of a gateway or approaches to a bridge.

bastion Projection from the general outline of a fortress from which the garrison can defend by flanking fire the ground before the ramparts. From the mid-sixteenth century generally a four-sided angled projection.

battery Any place where guns or mortars are mounted.

blockhouse Small detached fort at a strategic point, later often a wooden structure.

bulwark Early term for a bastion or blockhouse.

caponier Covered communication across a ditch leading to outworks, usually loopholed. Also a powerful casemated work projecting into or across a ditch to provide flanking fire.

Carnot Wall Detached wall at the foot of the rampart and separated from it by a *chemin des rondes*.

carronade Short piece of ordnance with a large bore but of different calibres. Chiefly used on shipboard.

casemate Bomb-proof vaulted chamber within the ramparts providing an emplacement for a gun and/or a barrack room.

cavalier Raised battery, usually built on a bastion to provide an additional tier of fire.

chemin des rondes Passage or sentry path at the top of the scarp wall with a parapet for cover.

citadel Self-contained fortress usually within a town's fortifications intended as a place of last resort and for control of the town.

counterscarp Exterior slope or revetment of a ditch.

counterscarp gallery Loopholed passage behind the counterscarp wall to defend the ditch.

covered way Continuous communication on the outer edge of the ditch protected by an earthwork parapet from enemy fire.

culverin Large cannon, very long in proportion to its bore which was in the region of 5in (127mm). Demi-culverin with a bore of *c.* 4in (100mm).

curtain Length of rampart between two bastions on the main line of a defensive work.

embrasure Opening in a parapet or wall through which a gun can be fired.

enceinte Also known as 'the body of the place'. The main defensive enclosure of a fortress excluding the outworks.

enfilade Fire coming from a flank which sweeps the length of the curtain or a fortification.

entrenched camp Protected area for the assembly or regrouping of an army.

escarp Outer slope or revetment of a rampart or inner slope of a ditch. Also scarp.

face (of a bastion) Outer sides of a work which meets at a salient angle projecting towards the field.

flank (of a bastion) Side of a work, usually a bastion, between the face and the curtain. The principal defensive element of a bastioned fortification.

flanker Battery mounted in the flank of a bastion from which flanking fire is directed across a curtain.

fort Position or building designed primarily for defence.

fougasse Small mine charged with explosive and rocks.

glacis Parapet of the covered way extended in a long slope to the field.

gorge Rear, whether open or closed, of any work. Usually the neck of a bastion or a detached work.

Haxo casemate Vaulted bomb-proof casemate for a gun built on the top of a rampart, invented by General Haxo.

keep Principal and strongest tower of a castle and the final point of defence.

line of defence Theoretical line drawn from the junction of a flank and a curtain to the salient of an adjacent bastion.

orillon Projection of the face of a bastion beyond the line of a retired flank, serving to protect a flanker.

palisade Obstacle of close-set pointed wooden stakes.

parapet Wall or earthen breastwork for the protection of troops on the forward edge of a rampart.

platform Hard surface of timber, stone etc. on which guns in battery can be placed.

postern A small entrance and tunnel leading out of a fortification.

rampart Mass of excavated earth on which the troops and guns of the garrison are raised and forming the main defence of the fortress.

ravelin Triangular, detached work with or without flanks in the ditch in front of a curtain and between two bastions.

redan Outwork consisting of two faces forming a salient angle.

redoubt Small enclosed work without bastions, sometimes in the form of a redan, either used as an outwork or placed inside a bastion or ravelin.

revetment Retaining wall of a rampart or for the sides of ditches.

salient An angle projecting outwards toward the field.

scarp See **escarp**

shoulder (of a bastion) Angle at the meeting of the face and the flank.

tenaille Low-lying work in the ditch between bastions for the protection of the curtain.

trace Plan of a fortified place and its angles of fire.

traverse Earthwork thrown up to bar enfilade fire along any line of a work which is liable to it.

work General term for any work of defence.

Places to visit

This is a list of those sites which are in the care of various public bodies or private trusts and where normally there is public access. It also includes some sites which are in private hands but where access is usually allowed upon application. The list is not exhaustive. Those sites in the care of English Heritage are marked with an asterisk.

Cornwall

Maker Heights
Five detached earthen redoubts across the Maker peninsula, near Plymouth, constructed in the late 1780s. Barracks built behind no. 2. By 1879 no. 4 had been converted to mount two, 12.5-inch guns and known as Grenville Battery.

Mount Edgcumbe Tower or **Barnpool Blockhouse**
Small, square, two-storeyed blockhouse of *c.* 1540 at the entrance to the Hamoaze and opposite the Devil's Point Blockhouse. In the grounds of Mount Edgcumbe Park, near Plymouth (Cornwall County Council).

*Pendennis Castle
Initial fortification was the small blockhouse of Little Dennis at the water's edge. The castle begun in 1540 was a circular gun tower; the polygonal curtain and gatehouse added later. Enclosed by an irregular bastioned trace in 1597. Half Moon Battery mounted two, 6-inch guns in World War II. Near Falmouth.

Polruan Blockhouse
Two-storey, square, masonry tower of the fifteenth century protecting the Polruan end of a chain boom across Fowey Harbour (Polruan Town Trust).

St Anthony Head
New battery for two, 6-inch guns constructed in 1897. Surrounded by a defensible earthwork. Near St Mawes. (National Trust).

*St Catherine's Castle
Small two-storey blockhouse at the entrance to Fowey Haven, built *c.* 1520.

St Ives – The Island
Bastioned earthwork with some granite revetment constructed in 1590s across the neck of the headland. Battery for three guns built 1854–6.

*St Mawes Castle
Architecturally the most decorative of all Henry VIII's castles with a round tower rising above three rounded bastions. Remains of a small blockhouse at the water's edge together with batteries of the 1780s. A battery for four, 12-pounder quick-firers of 1905 lies to the rear.

Devon

Brixham – Berry Head Batteries
Three extensive, detached batteries erected in 1779 and formerly armed with twenty 20-pounders, protected by an earthwork cutting off the headland (Torbay District Council).

*Dartmouth Bayards Cove
Small battery protected by a high wall and built 1509–10 to cover the entrance to the inner harbour.

*Dartmouth Castle
Innovative blockhouse begun in 1481 to guard the entrance to Dartmouth Haven. Contains large, square gunports for heavy guns at ground level. Its function was replaced in 1861 by a substantial casemated battery adapted for use in World War II.

Kingswear Castle
Opposite Dartmouth Castle and built a little later, in 1491, but shares many of Dartmouth's characteristics (Landmark Trust – by appointment).

Plymouth – Bovisand Fort.

On the eastern side of The Sound is a single-tier case-mated battery of the 1860s with remains of Staddon Point Battery on the cliff above (Bovisand Underwater Centre).

Plymouth – Crownhill Fort.

The centre and key of Plymouth's north-eastern land defences. A little altered example of the 1859 Royal Commission's forts with monumental architecture and impressive earthworks (Landmark Trust).

Plymouth – Devil's Point Blockhouse

Small seven-sided blockhouse of c. 1500, with two pairs of square gunports commanding the entrance to the Hamoaze.

Plymouth – Firestone Bay Blockhouse.

Seven-sided blockhouse, one of a number built along the water's edge of the Hoe in the early sixteenth century (Plymouth Corporation).

*Plymouth – Mount Batten Tower

Circular gun tower built in 1650s and commanding the Cattewater on the east side of Sutton Pool. Ten embrasures in the parapet.

*Plymouth – Royal Citadel

Large, irregular bastioned fort on the eastern side of the Hoe replacing a late sixteenth-century fort. Designed by Sir Bernard de Gomme and begun in 1665. Handsome baroque gate and some exteriors of internal buildings survive (in military occupation – guided tours only).

Plymouth – Western King Battery

Concrete gun positions of two, 12-pounder batteries from before World War I. In front, the brick emplacements for a pair of twin-6-pounder guns of World War II and searchlight positions in the cliff.

Salcombe Castle

Blockhouse constructed c. 1540 at the mouth of Salcombe harbour. A half-round tower towards the land is the principal surviving fragment.

Dorset

Brownsea Castle

Square, single-storey building with a hexagonal gun platform for the protection of Poole Harbour. Built in 1545–7 (National Trust – by appointment).

*Portland Castle

Henrician fort built in 1540 in association with Sandsfoot Castle to protect Weymouth Bay. Two-tier battery backed by a segmental two-storey barrack building.

Weymouth – Nothe Fort

A D-shaped casemated granite-faced fort for ten heavy guns begun in 1860 to complement the batteries on the Verne. Recent restoration (Weymouth Civic Society).

Weymouth – Sandsfoot Castle

Henrician castle. Octagonal battery almost entirely lost through cliff erosion. Tall, rectangular barrack block remains. Later bastioned earthwork enclosure to the rear (Weymouth District Council).

East Sussex

*Camber Castle

Large and elaborate Henrician castle originally protected a harbour now completely silted up. Castle in ruins but little altered since the sixteenth century. Near Rye.

Eastbourne Redoubt

One of two south-coast circular redoubts for eleven guns, associated with the Martello tower system, 1805–10. Military museum in the barrack casemates (Eastbourne District Council).

Eastbourne – Wish Tower

Martello tower no. 73. Now a museum of the Martello tower system.

Newhaven Fort

Constructed 1864–70 on the cliff to protect the newly developing port. Earthwork lower battery and large caponier at the foot of the cliffs linked by a tunnel from the fort above. Six-inch batteries operational during World War II. Military museum in the casemates (Lewes District Council).

*Pevensey Castle

Roman fort partly occupied by a medieval castle. World War II strongpoints and pillboxes built into the medieval and Roman ruins.

Seaford – Martello tower no. 74

Westernmost of the south-coast line of towers, now houses town museum.

Essex

East Tilbury, Coalhouse Fort

Large casemated fort built in 1860s as part of the Thames Advanced Line. Later 6-inch and 12-pounder guns mounted on the roof. Restoration in progress (Thurrock District Council).

Harwich Redoubt
Circular redoubt for eleven guns and part of the east-coast Martello tower system. Repaired by local trust.

*Tilbury Fort
Best example in the country of a late seventeenth-century fort of the Dutch School – double moat, ravelin and little-altered outworks. Riverside bastions and curtain modified in the late 1860s to take improved armament.

Hampshire

*Calshot Castle
Henrician castle of 1539/40 at the entrance to Southampton Water. Circular keep within a 16-sided curtain. Adapted in the nineteenth century.

Calshot – seaplane base
Royal Naval Air Service established here in 1913. Three early hangars survive (Hampshire County Council).

*Gosport – Fort Brockhurst
One of five polygonal forts comprising the 'Gosport Advanced Line' constructed 1858–62. Enclosed by a wide wet moat. The rear protected by a self-defensible circular keep.

Gosport – Gilkicker Fort
Detached, casemated D-shaped, granite-faced sea battery. In about 1900, 9.2-inch guns were mounted on top and an earth bank piled up against the seaward side of the granite wall (Hampshire County Council).

Gosport Lines
Traces of the eighteenth-century bastioned enceinte remain at the southern end of the town and to the north-east at Priddy's Hard.

*Hurst Castle
Part of the defences of the Needles Passage. Henrician castle with a twelve-sided keep surrounded by a curtain and three large rounded bastions. Long, casemated wing batteries for sixty-one guns were constructed either side of the Henrician castle in 1860s. Remains of twentieth-century batteries and fire-control positions on the roofs. Ferry from Keyhaven.

*Portsmouth – Fort Cumberland
At the south-east corner of Portsea Island, built between 1794 and 1820. The last major bastioned fortress to be constructed in England, unusual in combining a bastioned trace with use of casemated guns.

Portsmouth – Eastney Point
World War II anti-tank blocks, Port War signal station and defences of Langstone Harbour.

Portsmouth – Hilsea Lines
Bastioned lines across the north of Portsea Island defending the landward approaches, remodelled in 1860s (City of Portsmouth).

*Portsmouth – King James's Gate
Part of the seventeenth century town defences giving access from the Point. Its façade was removed to the United Services recreation ground *c.* 1860.

*Portsmouth – King's Bastion and Long Curtain
Last surviving stretch of the town defences as remodelled in the 1670s and 1730s (City of Portsmouth).

*Portsmouth – Landport Gate
The main entrance through the town's fortifications following their revision *c.* 1585. The present gatehouse was built in 1760.

Portsmouth – Fort Nelson
One of the line of detached forts on Portsdown Hill protecting Portsmouth from landward attack. Commenced 1861. Six-sided 'polygonal' fort. Now Royal Armouries museum of ordnance (Hampshire County Council).

Portsmouth – Point Battery
Adjacent to the Round Tower. Constructed in 1670s with eighteen casemates, modified and enlarged in 1847 (City of Portsmouth).

Portsmouth – Round Tower
Originally one of two towers on either side of the harbour entrance in the early fifteenth century. Much altered and refaced, heightened in the nineteenth century (City of Portsmouth).

Portsmouth – Southsea Castle
Built in 1544 as part of Henry VIII's scheme of coastal defence. Unusual in having a square tower with rectangular batteries to east and west linked by two angled salients. Remodelled in the 1670s and 1814; large wing batteries added in the 1860s. Now a museum (City of Portsmouth).

Portsmouth – Spitbank Fort
Northernmost of the Spithead sea-forts, built in the 1860s. Armoured on the seaward side, single tier of casemates over basement magazines (private – seasonal access).

Portsmouth – Square Tower
Built in 1494 as a gun tower, it became a magazine before

being adapted by the Victualling Board as a meat store. Top reinforced for 8-inch guns in 1848–50 (City of Portsmouth).

Portsmouth – Ten Gun Battery and Saluting Platform

Saluting Platform constructed early in the sixteenth century east of the Square Tower. Ten-Gun Battery part of the improvements of the seventeenth century (City of Portsmouth).

Portsmouth – Fort Widley

One of the line of detached forts on Portsdown Hill protecting Portsmouth from landward attack. Built in the 1860s. Six-sided polygonal fort with defensible barrack in the gorge (City of Portsmouth).

Isle of Wight

Bembridge Fort

Defensible barracks of the 1860s serving the batteries in the Sandown Bay area. Used for industrial functions (National Trust – by appointment).

*Carisbrooke Castle

Medieval castle converted into an artillery fortification 1585–8 and enveloped with a bastioned enceinte in 1596–7.

Golden Hill Fort

Defensible barracks built 1863–72 to serve the batteries of the Needles Defences. Hexagonal in plan with caponiers flanking the ditch. Now a holiday camp.

Needles Batteries

Old Needles Battery built 1861–3 for six, 7-inch guns. In 1889–92 subject to searchlight experiments to counter fast torpedo boats. New Needles Battery for 9.2-inch guns was built higher up the cliff in 1893–5 (National Trust).

Puckpool Mortar Battery

Part of the Spithead defences. Constructed 1863–5 for twenty-one, 13-inch mortars. Subsequently converted for heavy guns and in use during World War II (Ryde District Council).

Fort Victoria

Single tier casemated battery built 1852–6, later used as a submarine mining depot. Barracks demolished 1969 (Isle of Wight County Council).

*Yarmouth Castle

Last of the forts built by Henry VIII and the first surviving example of an Italianate orillon bastion flanking the landward sides.

Isles of Scilly

*St Mary's – Garrison Walls

Irregular and incomplete bastioned trace round the Hugh begun in the late sixteenth century, enlarged in the eighteenth. Early twentieth-century gun batteries on the hilltop.

*St Mary's – Harry's Walls

Unfinished Italianate bastioned fort built in 1551. The first of its kind to be planned in England.

St. Mary's – Star Castle

Built in 1593 for the defence of the island. Central building in the form of an eight-pointed star surrounded by a curtain wall of similar plan (hotel).

*Tresco – Cromwell's Castle

Tall, circular gun tower built *c.* 1650 to protect the anchorage of New Grimsby. Eighteenth century gun battery added near the water's edge.

*Tresco – King Charles's Castle

Built 1551–4 with hexagonal gun room with domestic accommodation behind. Badly sited for control of the harbour.

*Tresco Old – Blockhouse

Small blockhouse and gun platform built in the 1550s to protect Old Grimsby.

Kent

Chatham – Fort Amherst

The southern end of the Brompton Lines begun in 1756 to protect Chatham Dockyard, retrenched in the late eighteenth century to form Amherst Redoubt. In course of restoration (Fort Amherst and Lines Trust).

*Deal Castle

The largest and most powerful of all Henry VIII's 1539–40 scheme of coastal defence. Central circular keep has six small rounded bastions attached and these are surrounded by a curtain and six larger bastions and a moat. Converted into residence during eighteenth century.

*Dover – Archcliffe Fort

Part of the defences of Dover owing its origins to the time of Henry VIII. Bastioned landward front probably of early eighteenth century date. Not open to the public at present.

*Dover Castle

One of the great fortresses of Europe with its nucleus in the twelfth- and thirteenth-century castle. Considerably altered in the mid 1750s and enlarged during Napoleonic Wars. The batteries protecting the harbour were maintained during the nineteenth century and the castle was the headquarters for the Dover and Channel defences during both world wars.

*Dover – Drop Redoubt etc., Western Heights
The hill which dominates the west side of Dover was first fortified in 1779. Substantially strengthened in 1803–15 and again improved in the 1860s. The Drop Redoubt, North Centre bastion and the Citadel joined by continuous lines. The Grand Shaft, with triple stair, linked the now demolished barracks with the town below. Grand Shaft (Dover District Council).

Dover – St Martin's Battery, Western Heights
Three 6-inch gun battery with World War II gun-houses on the site of earlier batteries.

*Dymchurch – Martello tower no. 24
One of the 74 towers built along the south coast between 1805 and 1812. Small exhibition inside.

Gravesend Blockhouse
Excavated half of the D-shaped artillery blockhouse of 1539, one of five similar blockhouses guarding the Thames Estuary (in front of the Clarendon Royal Hotel).

Gravesend – New Tavern Fort
Battery built in 1778 to cross fire with Tilbury Fort opposite. Remodelled in 1868–9 for improved armament. Restored, with some guns remounted (Gravesend Corporation).

Hawkinge – Battle of Britain airfield/museum
Operations block, armoury, hangars etc. among the few surviving buildings associated with the grass airfield now in the process of development for housing.

Hythe – Royal Military Canal
Constructed in 1804 under the direction of Sir John Rennie as part of the anti-invasion measures linked to the Martello tower system.

Sheerness
Fragmentary remains of the seventeenth- and eighteenth-century dockyard defences. The massive two-tiered casemated Garrison Point Fort of the 1860s is not readily accessible but the early twentieth-century gun towers and batteries are visible from the waterfront.

Sheppey – Fletcher Battery
World War I battery for two, 9.2-inch guns together with fire-control buildings and remains of a defended perimeter commanded by pillboxes of unusual plan (private caravan park).

*Upnor Castle
Built in 1559–63 to protect the queen's ships moored in the Medway. Angle bastion projects into the river with a towered front of barracks over the river bank. Converted into a powder magazine after the Dutch raid of 1667. Barracks of 1719 nearby.

Upnor – Cockham Wood Fort
Eroded remains of a two-tiered battery constructed after the Dutch raid on the north bank of the Medway.

*Walmer Castle
South of Deal Castle and one of the three castles 'which keep the Downs'. Built in 1539–40 with a central, circular tower and outer ring of four large, rounded bastions. Converted in the eighteenth century as a marine residence for the Lords Warden of the Cinque Ports.

London

Whitehall – Cabinet War Rooms
Underground command centre serving the War Cabinet, Chiefs of Staff and the Commander-in-Chief Home Forces (Imperial War Museum).

Suffolk

*Landguard Fort
At the entrance to the Orwell Estuary, near Felixstowe. A pentagonal fort of the 1740s, substantially remodelled in 1870 with granite-faced casemates. Adjacent batteries improved or added to in both world wars.

West Sussex

Littlehampton Fort
Commanding the entrance to the River Arun. On the east side the rampart of a 1759 battery behind the lighthouse; on the west a bastioned-shaped fort of 1859 with a loopholed Carnot Wall below the ramparts.

Shoreham Redoubt
Built at the entrance to Shoreham Harbour in 1857. Bastion-shaped fort for six guns, barracks to rear now demolished. Carnot Wall in the ditch.

Shoreham airfield
First established in 1911. In use in both world wars.

Some wartime buildings still in use. A gunnery practice dome remains and the terminal belongs to 1930s.

Tangmere – aviation museum
Few buildings of the two world wars remain. Good site museum.

Channel Islands

Alderney
Many of the forts and batteries erected in the 1850s by Jervois are accessible. **Fort Clonque** owned by the Landmark Trust is used for holiday accommodation.

Guernsey

Pezerie Battery
Small coastal battery of unusual plan, reformed in 1804 for three 18-pounders.

Rocquaine – Fort Grey
Circular battery enclosing a round gun tower, constructed in 1803. Now a maritime museum (States of Guernsey).

St Peter Port – Castle Cornet
Medieval castle reconstructed in the sixteenth century as an irregular-bastioned artillery fort. Much of the medieval core destroyed in 1672 by a powder-magazine explosion yet remained an active fortification into the nineteenth century (States of Guernsey).

Jersey

Gorey – Mont Orgueil Castle
Medieval castle adapted in the fifteenth century for artillery but substantially remodelled 1537–50 (Jersey Heritage Trust).

Gorey – Victoria Tower
Circular gun tower built in 1837 as an advanced work for Mont Orgueil Castle.

St Helier – Elizabeth Castle.
Built on an island south of St Helier, the original core is the 'Upper Ward', a small irregular-bastioned fort of 1594–1601. Enlarged in the seventeenth century and in 1731–4 (Jersey Heritage Trust).

St Helier – Fort Regent
Irregular bastioned fort on the hill above St Helier built 1806–14 and superseded Elizabeth Castle. Interior now occupied by a leisure centre.

St Aubin's Bay – St Aubin's Fort
Tower built in 1542, remodelled in 1742 and again 1838–40. German casemates added 1940–5. A watersports centre.

St Ouen's Bay – Kempt Tower
Gun tower similar in appearance to the English south-coast Martello towers behind a three-gun battery and built in 1834. The bay was substantially fortified by the Germans in 1940–5 (Jersey Heritage Trust).

Further reading

Much has been written on British naval and military history, its admirals and generals, and the development of regiments and institutions. A great deal of this has focused on overseas battles and campaigns, the victories and defeats, heroism and sometimes incompetence. The more prosaic business of maintaining defences as a deterrent against raid or invasion of the British Isles has not received as much attention. The following list of books which do concern themselves significantly with home defence is selective but most of these publications have extensive bibliographies. They have been grouped under four main themes.

The threat of invasion

Fleming, Peter *Operation Sealion*. An account of the German preparations and the British counter-measures originally published as *Invasion 1940,* Rupert Hart-Davis, 1957; Pan Books, London, 1984

Glover, Michael *Invasion Scare 1940*, Leo Cooper, London, 1990

Glover, Richard *Britain at Bay: Defence against Bonaparte 1803–14,* Allen and Unwin, London, 1973

Gooch, John *The Plans of War: The General Staff and British Military Strategy, c. 1900–1916,* Routledge, London, 1974

Holland Rose, J. and Broadley, A.M. *Dumouriez and the Defence of England against Napoleon,* John Lane, London, 1909

Longmate, Norman *Island Fortress: The defence of Great Britain 1603–1945*, Hutchinson/Random Century, London, 1991

Mclynn, Frank *Invasion: From the Armada to Hitler, 1588–1945*, Routledge, London, 1987

Richmond, Admiral Sir Herbert W. *The Invasion of Britain: An account of plans, attempts and counter-measures from 1586 to 1918*, Methuen, London, 1941

Stuart Jones, E.H. *The Last Invasion of Britain*, University of Wales, Cardiff 1950

The Royal Navy and Home Defence

Baxter, James, Phinney *The Introduction of the Ironclad Warship*, Cambridge, Mass., 1968

Callender, Sir Geoffrey and Hinsley, F.H. *The Naval Side of British History 1485–1945*, Christophers, London, 1954

Coad, Jonathan *Historic Architecture of the Royal Navy: An introduction*, Scholar Press, London, 1989

Kennedy, Paul M. *The Rise and Fall of British Naval Mastery,* Macmillan Education, Basingstoke/London, 1983

Lewis, Michael *The Navy of Britain*, Allen and Unwin, London, 1948

Martin Colin and Parker, Geoffrey *The Spanish Armada*, London, 1988

Rodger, N.A.M. *The Insatiable Earl: A life of John Montagu, 4th Earl of Sandwich*, Harper Collins, London, 1993

Rogers, P.G. *The Dutch in the Medway*, Oxford University Press, Oxford, 1970

Temple Patterson, A. *The Other Armada: The Franco-Spanish attempt to invade Britain in 1779*, Manchester University Press, Manchester, 1960

The development of military engineering

Duffy, Christopher *Fire and Stone: The science of fortress warfare 1600–1860*, David and Charles, Newton Abbot, 1975

Duffy, Christopher S*iege Warfare: The fortress in the early modern world, 1494–1660*, Routledge and Kegan Paul, London, 1979

Duffy, Christopher *The Fortress in the Age of Vauban and Frederick the Great, Siege Warfare*, volume II, Routledge and Kegan Paul, London, 1985

Hale, Sir John R. *Renaissance Fortification: Art or engineering*, Thames and Hudson, London, 1977

Hughes, Quentin *Military Architecture: The art of defence from earliest times to the Atlantic Wall*, 2nd edn, Beaufort Publishing, Liphook 1991

Mallory Keith and Ottar, Arvid *Architecture of Aggression: A history of military architecture in north-west Europe 1900–1945*, Architectural Press, London, 1973

Sydenham Clarke, George *Fortification: its past achievements, recent developments and future progress*, Beaufort

Publishing, Liphook, 1989 (Facsimile reprint of 2nd edn, 1907)

Britain's defences

Ashworth, Chris *Action Stations 5: Military airfields of the south-west*, Patrick Stephens, Wellingborough, 1990.

Ashworth, Chris *Action Stations 9: Military airfields of the central south and south-east*, Patrick Stephens, Wellingborough, 1990).

Collier, Basil *The Defence of the United Kingdom,* History of the Second World War, United Kingdom Military Series, HMSO, London, 1957

Colvin, H M. (ed.) *The History of the King's Works, IV, 1485–1660* (Part II), HMSO, London, 1982.

Davies, William *Fort Regent*, privately published, St Helier, 1971.

Gander, Terry *Military Archaeology: A collector's guide to 20th century war relics*, Patrick Stephens, Cambridge, 1979

Goodwin, John *The Military Defence of West Sussex,* Middleton Press, Midhurst, 1985.

Hogg, Ian V. C*oast Defences of England and Wales 1856–1956*, David and Charles, Newton Abbot, 1974

Kent, Peter *Fortifications of East Anglia*, Terence Dalton, Lavenham, 1988.

Liddell Hart, B.H. *The Defence of Britain*, Faber and Faber, London, 1939

Maurice-Jones, Colonel K. W. *The History of Coast Artillery in the British Army*, Royal Artillery Institution, Woolwich, 1959

O'Brien, Terance *Civil Defence*, History of the Second World War, HMSO, London, 1955

Saunders, Andrew *Fortress Britain: Artillery fortification in the British Isles and Ireland,* Beaufort Publishing, Liphook, 1989

Smith, David J. *Britain's Military Airfields 1939–45*, Patrick Stephens, Wellingborough, 1989.

Smith, V.T.C. *Defending London's River: The story of the Thames forts 1540–1945*, North Kent Books, Rochester, 1985.

Sutcliffe, Sheila *Martello Towers*, David and Charles, Newton Abbot, 1972.

Vine, Paul A. L. *The Royal Military Canal*, David and Charles, Newton Abbot, 1972

Wills, Henry *Pillboxes: A study of UK defences 1940*, Leo Cooper/Secker and Warburg, London, 1985.

Woodward, F.W. *Plymouth's Defences: A short history*, privately published, Ivybridge, 1990

For fortifications and defence works in the care of English Heritage, National Trust, local authorities and private trusts, informative and well-illustrated handbooks are generally available.

Index

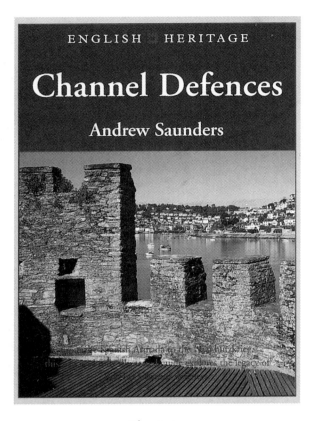

ENGLISH HERITAGE

Channel Defences

Andrew Saunders

The Author

Andrew Saunders is a specialist in military architecture of all periods and has excavated widely, including at Lydford Castle, Devon, and at Launceston Castle, Cornwall. He was Chief Inspector of Ancient Monuments and Historic Buildings (1973–89) for English Heritage and is President of the Royal Archaeological Institute, Chairman of the International Fortress Council and Chairman designate of the Fortress Study Group. He is the author of many books and articles.

'One of the great classic series of British archaeology.' *Current Archaeology*

This volume is part of a major series, jointly conceived for English Heritage and Batsford, under the general editorship of Dr Stephen Johnson at English Heritage.